P9-EDI-904

VITAL KNOWLEDGE FOR PROSPECTIVE PARENTS

*What the chances are of bearing a normal child after one or more miscarriages

*Whether sex during pregnancy increases the risk of miscarriage

*The current medical opinion about the use of hormones to prevent miscarriage

*How to select a doctor you can trust to give you the aid you want in facing possible complications in pregnancy

*At which stage of pregnancy a miscarriage is likely to occur

*And so much more comforting and up-to-date information about both the physiological and psychological impact of this difficult experience

ABOUT THE AUTHORS:

HANK PIZER is a medical writer and researcher who works as a physician's assistant. He is co-author of *The Post Partum Book* and *The New Birth Control Program*.

CHRISTINE O'BRIEN PALINSKI is a psychologist who has conducted many interviews with couples who have experienced miscarriages and with doctors specializing in problem pregnancies. She also has first-hand knowledge of the subject, having had three miscarriages herself between two successful pregnancies.

Medical Reference Books from SIGNET

COPING WITH A MISCARRIAGE

Why It Happens and How to Deal with Its Impact

by
Hank Pizer and
Christine O'Brien Palinski

A SIGNET BOOK

NEW AMERICAN LIBRARY

PUBLISHER'S NOTE

The ideas, procedures, and suggestions contained in this book are not intended as a substitute for consulting with your physician. All matters regarding your health require medical supervision.

Coping with a Miscarriage was also published in a Plume edition.

Drawings by Della O'Shea

This is an authorized reprint of a hardcover edition published by The Dial Press.

For Mark Palinski and Rita Keenan O'Brien

We are especially grateful to the women and men who shared their miscarriage experiences with us. We also thank the physicians and other medical professionals who took the time to be interviewed.

Contents

Foreword

Although miscarriage is a frequent occurrence among women, there are no good discussions of the topic written for the general public. I was thus very excited to read this book, which provides an excellent analysis of both the technical and emotional aspects of this difficult experience.

As a woman and as a physician, I continue to be influenced by the ideas developed in the 1960's and 1970's. I see a book such as this one, which discusses the facts and feelings around a previously untalked-about issue, as part of a current trend: a response to the initiative of the women's movement and a political force in itself. The women's movement has taught us that women have traditionally been powerless. In health care women have not had access to information concerning their bodies, and exploring and obtaining information has been hindered by cultural taboos. Thus the medical profession has maintained its power and control over many aspects of women's lives. To take that power back involves seizing control—first by obtaining information and then by sharing this information and the associated feelings with other women. An early and very significant example of this approach was the book *Our Bodies, Ourselves*. This was the beginning of many discussions and writings sharing technical

information, emotional responses, and a growing awareness
of the power that this brings.

Hank and Chris have also taken this approach. The chapters describing in lay-person's language what happens during
a miscarriage, the type of medical intervention, treatment,
etc., are essential both as explanations and as a demystifica-
tion of the human body and of what doctors really know and
can do. Equally important in this book, and often neglected
by the medical establishment, is the personal sharing of
emotional responses: the fear, the guilt, the impact on relationships and children. The power of information and of
encouragement to share one's feelings during times of crisis
cannot be underestimated. As prepared childbirth has vividly
taught us, the sharing of information and emotional and
physical preparation can markedly change the experience of
labor and birth. Similarly, people are learning that coping
with pain and death is easier in an open and supportive
environment.

A unique and significant contribution of this book is the
discussion of the responsibilities and reactions of men who
are involved in the miscarriage experience. It has often been
necessary for men to be excluded by women from their
growth process as women define their own needs and begin to
move toward greater self-awareness. This has stimulated many
men to reevaluate their own responses and assumptions, to
look at traditionally "masculine" behavior both in the light
of women's criticisms and in view of the benefits and costs to
the men themselves. This book, with its emphasis on men's
as well as women's feelings, thus represents an attempt to
reunite the two, to encourage men to express their grief and
pain, both for their own growth and for the benefit of the
women with whom they share their lives.

Hank and Chris touch upon several women's experiences
with their physicians. These experiences range from insensitive and brusque interchanges to more caring and compas-

sionate relationships. Though some women are able to find sensitive and supportive physicians, it is important to look carefully at the doctor-patient relationship. This interaction traditionally has been similar to the parent-child relationship. If the "parent" is a good parent, i.e., if the physician is attentive and caring, there is a tendency to idolize him or her. "He can do no wrong." While this reaction is very understandable, it has inherent risks: the patient is still "at the mercy" of the physician; the physician commands an inordinate amount of power and thus can misuse it.

In addition, the health-care provider is often not sensitive to the needs of the patient. This is partly an outgrowth of medical training which focuses primarily on the technology of medicine: how to make the diagnosis, what drug to give, when to operate, etc. In this context the emotional responses of the doctor and of the patient and the family are often lost. One of the major problems, as this book reveals, is that there is much that is unknown about many disease processes, such as miscarriage. The doctor often relies on intuition as much as on factual evidence. It is precisely because of this indeterminateness—combines with the patient's expectation that the doctor will be in charge and knowledgeable—that many doctors become defensive and insensitive to their own insecurities. In addition, to be "professional" often means to be unattuned to one's personal feelings. Obviously there are many problems with the traditional relationship between doctor and patient.

The dilemma is increased in obstetrics and gynecology, where much of the training is surgical—the most technological—and where 95 percent of the physicians are men and all of the patients are women. The struggles and conflicts that men and women are facing at work and at home are also potentially experienced in the doctor's office—issues of power, respect, and sensitivity.

So where does that leave us? There is much work to be

done. On a personal level, self-awareness and education can help women and men grow with each other and support each other through painful experiences as well as joyous ones. With the power that this brings it may then be possible to change the system, to make research on common medical emergencies a priority, to make sensitivity as valued as technical competence. This book takes a useful step in that direction.

Alice Rothchild, M.D.
Obstetrician/Gynecologist
Boston, Massachusetts
September 18, 1979

CHILDBIRTH & MISCARRIAGE

I

Chris's Experience

Miscarriages are more common than most of us realize. Hundreds of thousands occur each year, yet it is a silent problem. This silence accounts for the bewilderment, shock, and fear that many people feel when they miscarry for the first time. Such a lack of information is typical even of women who have experienced second and third miscarriages.

Chris Palínski had had three miscarriages when she approached Hank Pizer about writing a book on the subject. Together we decided to share her own personal knowledge and his medical knowledge with the many couples who have to confront this problem. Chris tells her own story in the first person. Our joint knowledge and perspective is presented in more general terms.

It was a little over three years ago that my husband, Mark, and I decided (rather naively) to have a second child. We had had one child without any real difficulties. My pregnancy had been normal, and I had worked through most of it. Our daughter Suze was nearly four years of age at the time and would be closer to five when her sibling arrived, which seemed all right. It was also a good time for us. Mark was finishing his physician's-assistant training, and I was working as a high-school counselor. We planned the birth to coincide with the end of the school year and joyfully announced my pregnancy to our families and friends and, of course, Suze, as I entered my third month.

Only a few weeks later we were stunned by my miscarriage. I noticed some slight spotting one Saturday but at that time wasn't at all alarmed. I'd never considered the possibility of any difficulty with the pregnancy and didn't know anyone my age who had miscarried. When the spotting continued through Monday, I called my obstetrician's office, still not concerned that there was any major problem. The nurse I spoke with told me to come right in. When I said that I was working and couldn't come immediately, she told me that they wouldn't be responsible for my condition unless I came right over. That was when I began to be alarmed.

I left my office at school and went directly to his office. Unfortunately my own physician wasn't there, so I had to see one of his associates. He examined me and said, "Mrs. Palinski, you are aborting. Go home and rest. Call if cramps start, otherwise come back tomorrow." No ifs, no maybes, just the flat statement that I was "aborting," and then he left the room.

I was shocked, frightened, and terribly sad. I sat on the examining table crying for a while. Then a sympathetic nurse came in to help me on with my clothes, and I left. I sobbed all the way home and sat in my kitchen all afternoon with a dear friend, who is a nurse and women's-health specialist and who was mercifully nearby. She held my hand and cried with me and explained things and generally took care of me that day, a shared experience which will bond us forever. She told me what to expect—the cramping and the bleeding—which would increase until I passed the fetus. When I was talked out, she left. Later that night I had twenty minutes of very uncomfortable cramping, like contractions during birthing, and heavy bleeding. By morning it was obviously all over. I saw my physician that morning, and he told me very quickly that I had "aborted." I remember his use of that term in place of *miscarriage* was a bit unsettling.

The doctor talked with me awhile about the probable cause, about my feelings, and about the D and C (dilation and curettage) that he recommended as our next step. He arranged to meet me at the hospital an hour later. I called Mark, who met us there and stayed with me while I was prepped and examined and through the D and C. Two hours later it was over, and I was riding home groggy and spent. In just over twenty-four hours *everything* had changed.

I was quite depressed and withdrawn for several days afterward. I had found a new and frightening mistrust for my body, which was extremely unpleasant. However, as I am basically a survivor and a positive person, I threw myself into the task of "solving" the problem. In the next few months I looked everywhere I could for information about miscarriage. I found very little. There weren't *any* books available even in the most extensive libraries. A few short paragraphs in books on pregnancy was the best that I could do.

Even Mark and my friends in the medical field found little in the medical libraries. Their message, and that of my doctor, was to accept the miscarriage as a kind of protective natural intervention which occurs in 15 to 20 percent of all pregnancies. I accepted this and looked forward to the next pregnancy, which would erase this misery.

I became pregnant a few months after the first miscarriage, as the doctor had advised. At that time I was only cautiously optimistic. We didn't tell Suze or many other people, and during this pregnancy I tried to do all the right things for my body. I was careful about my diet; I didn't smoke or drink. I cut back on my activity, got lots of rest, and even cut my working days from five to three. I had been living with some guilt and fear that something I had done during the earlier pregnancy had caused the failure, so I tried to be especially careful.

In spite of all the special treatment that I was giving myself, the pregnancy only lasted twelve weeks. As soon as I started spotting I knew I would miscarry, but I spent nearly a week in bed waiting. Eventually the cramps began—much more severe this time—and I went to the hospital. I spent approximately twelve hours in labor, passing lots of blood and feeling a lot of pain, before I actually took any medication. I have vivid memories of the pain.

I had to wait another twelve hours before getting a D and C again. I didn't know it then, but the Roman Catholic hospital I went to required a negative pregnancy test before they would perform the D and C (regardless of other symptoms). The wait was very upsetting, and I decided not to return to a Catholic hospital if I was ever faced with a miscarriage again. This second miscarriage in less than six months left me more depressed and more frightened about my chances of having another child.

I am not sure why Mark and I did not immediately have a series of tests done to find out right then what was wrong. We both wanted to have another child very much, and we did want answers. Our obstetrician's point of view was that since we had one normal child already, the available testing wouldn't offer us much information. Testing is often oriented toward the problems of couples who have not been able to reproduce at all. The medical advice we were given was generally encouraging; our doctor told us that we were still in a very good range statistically to produce a normal pregnancy. Our decision was to wait for a few months and then try again.

When I became pregnant about six months later, optimism

was hard to come by. I hadn't really found any tangible scientific information that helped me with my feelings. By then every little ripple in my pregnant body frightened me. I was even superstitious about repeating experiences I associated with earlier miscarriages.

This fourth pregnancy lasted four months. The familiar spotting, waiting, and contractions were followed, quickly this time, by a D and C. Once again it was all over. The process this time took seven days.

I knew then that I would not risk another replay of those events without a serious medical evaluation. We stayed with our obstetrician because we both liked and trusted him, and we began a series of tests immediately. While I was still in the hospital after the D and C, they drew blood samples for thyroid testing. The next day I had a glucose-tolerance test for diabetes.

Over the next few months both Mark and I went through several other tests, including genetic analysis and a urological evaluation. All along the way the specialists warned me not to hope for any answers. By then I was hostile toward all of them. "Why don't they know anything?" I thought. "And why isn't any research being done?" I felt that my future was in very detached, uninterested hands. It was an extremely tense period for me and for Mark.

The last step in the whole series of tests involved the culturing of tissue from my cervix and uterus to examine for infectious diseases. The results came back from the state health department—*positive!* They had identified the T-strain mycoplasma—something like a virus—in my uterus. My obstetrician called to explain to me that this T-strain mycoplasma had only recently been associated with both infertility and miscarriage.

We sent new cervical smears from me and urine from both Mark and me to the lab for treatment determination. The report indicated that one of the tetracyclines would cure my infection. Although there was no indication that Mark was also infected, he and I both took the course of antibiotics and were "cured."

Naturally we were overjoyed to have identified any problem that could be treated, although the doctor was careful to say that we couldn't be sure that the mycoplasma was the source of the problem. He was encouraged; we were encouraged and very much relieved. We decided to risk another try, in spite of the lack of certainty about the mycoplasma issue. By that time we were speculating about the possibility of doing this book, and we were already reading and researching the subject extensively. The more information Hank unearthed, the more we realized that this mycoplasma business was anything but definite.

I found that I was pregnant in the fall of 1978 and spent a very anxious winter. It wasn't until Christmas time, when I was too large to fit into my own clothes and people on the street were noticing my pregnancy, that I began to feel that this one was going to continue. As had been the case in the last two pregnancies, I was very careful about diet, rest, and exertion. The one factor that I was not able to control was my anxiety, which thankfully began to subside in the early spring. The pregnancy was completely normal—no spotting, no cramps. The baby became noticeably active in early December and continued to be extremely physical throughout my pregnancy, including the day of delivery. The later part of the pregnancy was a very happy, close time for Mark, Suze, and me, in spite of my increasing bulk and discomfort.

On April 29, the exact due date, at 10:36 P.M. our son, John William, was born. My labor was short and hard—less than three hours of noticeable contractions. The last hour moved so quickly that John beat our obstetrician to the delivery. Our plans for a Leboyer birth (low lights, silence, a gentle bath for the newborn immediately after birth) were scrapped when a rather surprised obstetrics resident was hurriedly summoned to "catch" the baby! It was, of course, exciting and wonderful. My only disappointment was that our obstetrician, Fred Storm, who had seen us through the past two years, wasn't there for those special moments.

Our son was healthy and active from the first seconds. He roomed in with me at the hospital and was pleasant to care for right away. A bout with jaundice a few days after we came home has been the only blot on his perfect record, and he seems to have recovered from that common though frightening problem. He is six weeks old now; as I type these words I'm listening with the proverbial "one ear" for him to awaken from his afternoon nap.

My experiences over the past two and a half years have been painful and difficult. A portion of that difficulty came from the lack of support available for women who miscarry. Although my obstetrician is a kind, humane, sensitive person who was able to communicate with me on this level, he had little to offer in the long run. I saw him when I was in crisis, and he was empathetic at those moments. But he wasn't there for my grieving later, and he wasn't there on a day-to-day basis.

Other women were my primary source of support. They seemed to be able to relate to my pain in ways that even Mark, who was feeling his own loss, couldn't. I had difficulty finding women my age who had miscarried, although I knew several people who had elected to abort. In my mother's age group, among her friends, I found many more women with firsthand experience of miscarriage. They were very supportive.

With some searching I found some peers, too. However, even at 32, many of my friends have not yet had children. It was hard for me to believe the 20-percent theory—that one out of five pregnancies terminates in a miscarriage. Few people seemed to talk about it, even if they had had the experience.

I searched for things to read in the popular literature, in medical books, in women's magazines, but met with nothing but frustration. The medical articles were in a jargon of their own and didn't offer me *answers,* in spite of the inside track I had, with my husband and several close friends in the medical profession.

I know what a comfort it would have been *the first time* to sit and read the information that took me two years to accumulate. It wasn't only the 20-percent theory and the why of my problem that I wanted to know more about, but also the feelings of others who had had or were having similar difficulties. All in all I was very much alone with my emotions.

Most women fortunately do not have to experience three miscarriages; but a steady percentage do have to deal with one or two during their childbearing years. It is for these women and their partners and families that I wanted to write a book—to share my experiences, my information, and to give encouragement.

The facts about miscarriage aren't as clear as we would wish them to be. It isn't high on the list of priorities in medicine nowadays, but we will present what is known and, in doing so, try to allay your fears as well as fill in the informational gaps in your experience. We believe that knowledge of the facts makes the reality more bearable.

Our approach will be to mix the factual, technical data with the personal, so that the information has a context as did my experience. We will remind you throughout the book that the miscarriage itself probably will not damage you in any physical way and that you will be very likely to have successful future pregnancies. This is true even after a number of miscarriages.

We will also place a lot of emphasis on the affective, or emotional, component of the miscarriage. Our experience has indicated that this area is badly neglected for most couples. A miscarriage is a frightening and depressing event. It is normal to respond with a certain amount of self-doubt, frustration, and anger. The sadness and grief can be overwhelming for couples who are really eager to have a child. The hurt subsides in time, but it is natural and healthy to feel it and especially important to express it.

This stress can be an opportunity for growth within yourself and within your relationship with your mate. You may never have thought much about the fallibility of your own body, about death, or even about your reproductive capacity before, but all are very real issues in life. In our own ways we all are forced to deal with them after a miscarriage. We hope you will find the sharing of these aspects of the experience through excerpts from our interviews helpful and comforting.

You will also learn about your body. We are often ignorant of our bodies' functioning until some problem arises. Yet this information is part of self-awareness, and it, too, promotes growth. We will try to be more clear and direct than the textbooks we've all seen in describing the biology of reproduction and the accidents that may happen along the way.

Having a family is important, but it doesn't always come easily. As with many important experiences in life—like education, a career, interpersonal relationships—fulfillment comes after some struggle. If you stay with it, you will probably have your family and will bring to them what you have learned from your disappointment and adjustment. The message is that you can learn from the hard times as well as the good times, and we hope that our book can give you some of the tools with which to make the necessary adjustments.

II

Definitions

I remember how taken aback I was when the doctor said, "Mrs. Palinski, you are aborting." I had always thought of an abortion as a medical procedure—with grave ethical and legal overtones—by which women voluntarily terminated their pregnancies. My pregnancy, however, was very much desired, and there was nothing voluntary about what was happening.

I had no idea of what was really going on in my body, except that I knew my pregnancy wasn't going to succeed. I did not know whether I would be sick, whether I would be able to have other children, whether those children would be normal, or even what a miscarriage really was.

What was I *mis-carrying* anyway? Had I done something wrong to cause this? I realized then that I knew very little about what was happening to my body and that I would have to begin to learn a whole lot more before it would make any sense at all.

WHAT IS A MISCARRIAGE?

In general, miscarriage is a loaded word, spoken in hushed
tones by one woman to another. Few people are clear about
its meaning. Miscarriage and spontaneous abortion (really
synonymous terms) are very alienating and frightening words
to many people. As a result it is hard to think clearly about
the medical problem until the negative social connotations of
the term are swept aside.

A miscarriage is a lay person's term for a *spontaneous
abortion*, which means that there is a premature delivery of a
fetus before it can survive on its own. In some hospitals such
a premature delivery before the eighteenth week is called a
spontaneous abortion; after that it is called a stillbirth if the
fetus cannot live on its own. The World Health Organization
defines a spontaneous abortion as a premature delivery of a
non-viable fetus before the twenty-eighth week. In either case
we consider these premature deliveries that result in a non-
viable fetus to be spontaneous abortions. It is different from
an *elective abortion* (induced abortion) in that it is not planned
and not voluntary. It happens on its own without drugs, an
operation, or any other medical procedure.

Thus, all preconceptions aside, a miscarriage is actually
early, spontaneously initiated childbirth. It is an active process,
not a forgetful or passive action. You do not *mis-carry* anything. In fact, carrying a baby to term involves a complex
interaction of mother and baby. If there is a problem in either
system, there is a potential for a miscarriage.

We would like to emphasize two important concepts:

1. A spontaneous abortion means that you and your
   mate are fertile. You were able to conceive. This is
   a very important fact, because it makes you much
   more likely to have a child than parents who do have
   a fertility problem.

2. Something happened very early in your pregnancy to cause the premature delivery of the baby before it could live on its own. When you pass the fetus, what you are actually feeling is labor, much like that of childbirth. The delivery is by muscular contractions of your uterus, combined with dilation (opening) of your cervix.

Since the subject is not often discussed openly, the real causes of early labor are widely misunderstood. Chapters 5 and 6 will be devoted to the causes of spontaneous abortion. The following are *not* known to be causes of miscarriage:

- Use of an oral contraceptive (birth-control pill)
- Prior use of an intrauterine device (IUD)
- Previous gonorrhea or other venereal disease, or pelvic inflammatory disease (PID)
- A previous elective abortion (except for the rare case of an incompetent cervix, discussed later)
- In general, horseback riding, working, or exercising
- Sexual intercourse, in any position, during pregnancy

There are many reasons for this early labor. Some have to do with problems with the fetus, and some have to do with the mother. It is currently thought that many spontaneous abortions are caused by problems with the baby's genes (basic life structure), inherited from the parents. For this reason a spontaneous abortion can be caused by a genetic problem of one or both of the parents. The genetic abnormality may be due to a chance event, or it may be caused by the basic genetic structure of the parents. We will treat this subject in detail in Chapter 5. We all inherit a certain number of "problem" genes from our parents. Sometimes these problems are never expressed ("silent" or recessive genes), sometimes they are minor (like nearsightedness), and occasionally they are fatal to the fetus.

Many factors evidently can cause early labor. In some cases the hereditary structure of one or both parents is defective. Other times chance genetic abnormalities occur that can precipitate a miscarriage. In a relatively small number of cases the mother cannot carry a baby due to anatomical problems or the presence of infection.

It is important to remind yourself that a miscarriage is really the *delivery* of a premature baby that probably would not be normal and could not live on its own. It does *not* mean that you have done something wrong that "caused" the miscarriage. I only came to accept this after much self-doubt and frustration, however, and it may be difficult for you or your mate to take much comfort from this realization right away. Certainly any fears and guilt feelings you might still have will not vanish overnight. It is all too easy for us to feel guilty about our hurts in life, especially if we are powerless to do anything about them.

HOW OFTEN DO MISCARRIAGES OCCUR?

It is estimated that between 15 and 20 percent of all pregnancies terminate in a spontaneous abortion. That means that about 300,000 miscarriages occur each year in the United States.

Though I never really *believed* that there could be so many miscarriages when I first heard the figure, I have now come to believe that it is accurate. Most people do not talk about their miscarriage experiences, and thus we are not aware of it when it happens to our friends or family. It took me a long time to begin to talk about it with my friends, and only then did I find other women my age who had also had spontaneous abortions. Moreover, after many conversations with my mother,

I now know that women of her generation often had miscarriages as well.

Because it happens so often, it is considered a normal variation in the pregnancy process. Some medical scientists have hypothesized that *more* than one out of five pregnancies end in spontaneous abortion. Probably many miscarriages occur so early in pregnancy that women do not know that they are pregnant. These *silent* miscarriages take the form of late and heavy periods after an unusually long menstrual cycle.

It is very common for a woman to have experienced such a "late" period. Often she passes a lot of blood and some tissue, accompanied by unusually severe cramping. We pass off these events without really thinking about them, but it is reasonable to assume that sometimes they are spontaneous abortions. Because we get our menstrual period, we do not consider the possibility of having been pregnant.

Age, occupation, and your life experience also seem to have some bearing on the frequency of spontaneous abortions. You are more likely to have a miscarriage as you get older. The risk of miscarriage increases as a woman gets older, for example; but the man's age is probably also a factor, though this has not been documented nearly as well. The studies referred to below were concerned exclusively with the age of the woman.

This does not mean you cannot have children, even if you are somewhat older when you begin to try to conceive. In one study the ages of women who spontaneously aborted ranged from 20 to 43, with the average age just over 29 years. In another often-quoted study the average age was 33 years. The average age of childbearing for women in the general population is somewhat lower than both these figures.

There is no special cut-off year in which you become too old to try to have a child. But with each successive year your chances for having a miscarriage do go up somewhat. Here are some sample figures to give you an idea of how your chances of spontaneously aborting do increase as you get older.

AGE	PERCENTAGE OF SPONTANEOUS ABORTIONS
20	12 percent
25	15 percent
30	17 percent
36	22 percent
40	31 percent
42	41 percent

It is important to note here that most research on older women who have children has been limited by small population size and inadequate studies until recently. Now that many couples are waiting longer to have children, we will get a better idea of the effect of age on the incidence of miscarriage. Even assuming that these statistics are reliable, a 40-year-old woman still has better than a two out of three chance of carrying a baby to term.

Your chances of having a miscarriage also increase if your work exposes you to certain chemicals, X rays or other radiation, and other stresses. During wartime and in situations where mothers are very undernourished, miscarriages occur more often. How often is hard to judge, since figures for populations under stress, such as war and famine, are hard to establish accurately.

To date there have been no studies describing the incidence of spontaneous abortion in women exposed to radiation from nuclear power plants. We can expect that such research will be undertaken, now that the nuclear issue has been raised on a national scale. Studies of mice exposed to low doses of radiation have demonstrated both mutation and fetal death (leading to spontaneous abortion), so we know that a danger may very well exist for humans as well.

There is some evidence that chemicals, for instance vinyl chloride, can cause fetal death and spontaneous abortion. Hard scientific data on humans is once again lacking. Interviews of workers exposed to vinyl chloride uncovered the fact that these workers did have an increased number of fetal deaths, but follow-up with regard to spontaneous abortions is very meager. Animal studies, however, point to the dangers of these chemicals to the developing fetus, and we must consider it prudent to avoid exposure to any chemical or drug during pregnancy. Early death or derangement of the normal growth pattern of the fetus can cause a spontaneous abortion.

WHEN DO MISCARRIAGES OCCUR?

Most spontaneous abortions occur very early in pregnancy, somewhere between the seventh and fourteenth week. This is somewhat variable and often hard to fix exactly. But many studies have confirmed this pattern. Most miscarriages happen when the fetus is very small and just beginning to form.

This has been recognized for quite some time. It alerted researchers to the notion that the high incidence of spontaneous abortions early in pregnancy might be due to problems with the fetus. In the early weeks of pregnancy the fetus and mother interact, sending important biological signals to each other. In some cases when the infant is not normal, these signals are not sent. These abnormal infants are then rejected early in pregnancy as nature's way of preventing abnormal births. This may also be caused by abnormalities in the mother's system, but we do not know the exact mechanism by which the rejection process occurs; immunological and hormonal research in this area may someday provide us with better answers. The point is that the mother's body is not entirely responsible, so you should not try to put all the blame on yourself.

A pregnancy is dated by subtracting two weeks from the total number of weeks since the last menstrual period. The theory behind this method of estimation is quite simple. Most women ovulate about 14 days before their *next* menstrual period. Moreover, most women have cycles that are between 26 and 33 days long. By subtracting 14, the day of ovulation (and hence of conception) is placed somewhere between day 11 and 18 after the first day of your last menstrual period. For the purposes of estimating the length of time you had been pregnant when the spontaneous abortion occurred, a difference of a few days is not important.

There is no magic week after which you are ''safe'' from having a miscarriage. But we can say with some certainty that most spontaneous abortions happen before the sixteenth week of pregnancy. We do not know the exact reason why four months of pregnancy seems to be a cut-off time for most of these events, but study after study has confirmed this.

It is useful to make a distinction between *early* spontaneous abortions and *late* (between the seventeenth and twenty-eighth week). It is thought that these two types of miscarriage have different underlying causes, and they are treated with different medical therapies. Because of these differences it is important that the number of weeks that you were pregnant be established.

EARLY SPONTANEOUS ABORTIONS

For most parents, then, the miscarriage occurs sometime between the seventh and fourteenth week of pregnancy, just as they are beginning to enjoy the idea of having a child. It is sad that it comes at such a crucial time, for this early period in pregnancy is often the happiest for the couple. It is a time of expectation, plans, and strong interpersonal bonds. It is no wonder that a miscarriage comes as a terrible shock.

These early spontaneous abortions are commonly caused by genetic abnormalities in the baby. There is a demonstrable genetic problem in about half of these cases; the causes of the others are generally not clear. Since the percentage of abnormalities is so high, it is important for parents to realize that their miscarriage may be saving them the years of stress that raising an abnormal child involves. Chapter 5 deals with the genetic issue in detail and Chapter 6 with other causes.

LATE SPONTANEOUS ABORTIONS

Late spontaneous abortions generally involve normal fetuses, and the precise cause of them remains quite a mystery. These abortions are not thought to be caused by accidents or injuries to the mother. There is generally also no obvious relationship to any source of infection or offending chemical agent.

In late spontaneous abortions the placenta detaches from the wall of the uterus and the fetus is passed through the cervix and vagina, thereby being delivered prematurely. Because the cervix, or mouth of the uterus, must open for the fetus to pass, it has been hypothesized that these late spontaneous abortions are caused by a problem with the cervix—an *"incompetent cervix"* is the current terminology.

Whether or not the cervix is really incompetent is actually open to debate. However, there are surgical procedures which strengthen the cervix and are often successful in helping women carry their babies to term. There are certain anatomical abnormalities in the uterus that have been linked to these late miscarriages. Chapter 6 will discuss this whole subject in more detail.

MORE THAN ONE MISCARRIAGE?

If you have had one spontaneous abortion it is very understandable that you should worry and wonder about your chances of having two, three, four, or even more spontaneous abortions. There are some studies that can give us an idea of the likelihood of your repeating your miscarriage, and the figures should provide you with some hope and optimism.

Although the various studies show slightly different statistical results, we can summarize them as follows:

- If you have had one spontaneous abortion, your likelihood of having a second one goes up either very slightly or not at all. Thus you are still about as likely to have another miscarriage as any other couple in the general population, i.e. 15-20 percent.
- After two spontaneous abortions your chance of having a third increased somewhat from that of the general population. At that point you stand about a one in three (33 percent) chance of having another miscarriage; that is, you have a *two to one* chance of having a normal, full-term baby, even after two consecutive spontaneous abortions.
- After three spontaneous abortions your chance of having a fourth goes up again. At that point you seem to have about a 50-50 chance of having another miscarriage.

Reliable studies of women who have had more than three spontaneous abortions do not exist. That is probably because most of these women go on to have children, and the problem is ultimately resolved. As one obstetrician pointed out:

You don't see studies of couples who have had eight or nine spontaneous abortions because that is a very rare occurrence. Most people are successful in having a baby long before that.

Another point that we need to emphasize is that so-called spontaneous aborters—people who have miscarriages—are highly fertile. They are generally able to become pregnant rather quickly after their miscarriages. In this they are quite fortunate, because the infertile couple stands a much poorer chance of eventually carrying a normal baby to term. Moreover, the long periods that infertile couples wait before becoming pregnant are often emotionally quite trying.

There is some debate about how soon after miscarrying the couple should try to become pregnant again. Some obstetricians advise women who have repeated miscarriages to wait until they have had a few normal menstrual cycles before trying to become pregnant again. This provides time for some medical testing and, some think, for the formation of a healthy inner lining of the uterus (endometrium). However, there is little scientific evidence to indicate that it takes any more than one cycle to build up a normal lining. In this matter, these doctors are relying on intuition rather than on medical facts.

Even after a number of miscarriages you are still very likely to have a normal baby. Most studies indicate that a couple who had had a miscarriage has essentially the same chance as any other couple of producing a normal baby. Some studies even indicate that they are *more* likely than the average couple to have a normal baby, possibly because the woman's body has a proven mechanism (the spontaneous abortion) for rejecting genetic abnormalities. While all this data is not well validated at this point, there is little to indicate that couples who have one or two miscarriages are more likely to have an abnormal child than anyone else. Thus, if you do carry a baby to term, you should be confident that it is probably going to be a normal one.

SUMMARY

1. If you have had one or even a number of spontaneous abortions (miscarriages), you are not very unusual. It is a very common problem in pregnancy, and about one in five pregnancies ends in miscarriage.
2. A miscarriage is an active process, much like the labor of childbirth, in which the fetus is expelled from the uterus.
3. Because about 50 percent of miscarried fetuses are abnormal, it is thought that the spontaneous abortion is nature's method of preventing abnormal babies from being born.
4. It is thought that most miscarriages, at least those that occur within the first four months of pregnancy, are caused by genetic problems or infections and not just by problems with the mother's body. These are called *early* spontaneous abortions.
5. Late spontaneous abortions occur between the seventeenth and twenty-eighth week of pregnancy. They are believed to be caused by different factors than early abortions and have different medical treatments.

III

The Impact
of a Miscarriage

When I learned that I was aborting, I realized that I had little or no idea of what to expect. My doctor did not and probably could not tell me what it would feel like and what I would be going through. I had no idea what the pain would be like, what I should expect from my body, or what I would see passing out of my vagina.

There is a saying, Anticipation is worse than realization. It was certainly true for me and is probably true for just about everyone who goes through a miscarriage. My mind raced to the improbable and the disastrous. The more I sat alone in my kitchen, the more fear penetrated me and my thoughts extended to the worst.

It wasn't until my friend, the nurse, came and told me what to expect that I settled down a bit. I was still frightened, but she put things in perspective. Not only did she tell me what was going on inside my body, but she told me what I would probably be feeling during the day and night. I remember

34

taking all of that in and later gauging my experience against her descriptions. Knowing what to expect helped me a lot while I was bleeding, cramping, and passing the fetus.

SIGNS OF A MISCARRIAGE

Vaginal bleeding is the cardinal sign of the onset of spontaneous abortion. While your body may give you other signs as well, it is important to take any vaginal bleeding during pregnancy very seriously.

The bleeding usually starts with spotting, but sometimes it may be actual bleeding with cramping. By "spotting" we mean just that—a drop or two of blood on your underpants every few hours. Sometimes you spot for a few days and stop, and then go on to have a normal pregnancy. Some spotting is the prelude to heavier bleeding, cramping, and eventual passing of the fetus. The amount of bleeding you have has little relationship to what happens later. Some women who bleed a lot carry the baby successfully to term, while some women who have only experienced spotting will eventually miscarry. Physicians can recount stories of women who bled profusely, even required a blood transfusion (although this is very rare), but who went on to have normal full-term babies. There certainly is no rule, except that a miscarriage occurs in conjunction with vaginal bleeding. (In Chapter 6 we will discuss the causes of spotting that does not result in miscarriage.)

Studies have shown that about half of the women who bleed during pregnancy actually miscarry. The exact numbers are again difficult to set accurately, since many women who both bleed and miscarry are never included in any medical study. However, as a general rule the information leads us to the conclusion that you have a 50-50 chance of carrying your baby successfully, even if you have had vaginal bleeding.

What you may or may not feel is cramping. To expel the fetus your body must "push" it out with some degree of muscular contraction. For some women these contractions are very slight, while for others they are strong and painful, like labor.

All three of my miscarriages happened around the same stage in pregnancy, and yet the amount of bleeding and cramping differed substantially in all three. The first time, I spotted for a few days and then experienced about half an hour of uncomfortable cramping, during which time I passed a lot of clots and (I think) tissue (although I couldn't identify that). The other two miscarriages followed a week or more of spotting and involved long hours of difficult labor, more difficult in fact than the labor I experienced before the birth of my daughter, Suze.

I have since learned from my own experience, and from talking with other women, that there are no formulas for describing the physical sensations of a miscarriage. Every woman's experience is unique. Some women have slow, painful miscarriages, while others are barely aware of any physical discomfort at all. However, except for those women who have silent miscarriages and who do not realize that they are miscarrying, you always know that something is wrong. The bleeding and cramping are the most obvious signs. But that "something wrong" feeling may be subtle. You may feel some unusual fatigue, nausea, or other vague symptoms.

BEING AFRAID

It is very normal to be frightened when you see the first sign of bleeding. Some women are not alarmed—I was not the first time—but that is an uncommon reaction. I waited awhile before calling the doctor and was very shocked when the office nurse said, "We can't be responsible for you unless you come in right away." Having a menstrual period every month makes us somewhat used to vaginal bleeding, but in this case more concern on my part would have been appropriate.

If you do become frightened, consider it the normal response. As Dr. Henry Klapholz, a high-risk-obstetrics specialist pointed out:

> When a woman tells me that she is spotting, I come and see her in the emergency room, or she comes to my office right away. I always assume that there is some fear there—some fright that the woman is having. Most women who bleed understand that it is a possible miscarriage, and I want to see them right away. I have an emotional attachment to my patients, and I know that it is important to see them right away.
>
> I tell them that spotting in early pregnancy is a very common occurrence. It occurs in one fourth to one half of all pregnancies, and of those that bleed, some one half go on to miscarry. It is important that you understand that, number one, if you miscarry, it is not going to kill you or make you sick, and you'll probably be able to have as many children as you want afterwards. I usually say that if it is a first or second miscarriage.
>
> Second, there is nothing we can do at this point. It is really in nature's hands—or God's hands, if you will. But whatever happens, you will be all right. You won't be harmed, you won't be injured, your reproductive health won't be altered.

In spite of any amount of reassurance it is natural to be very frightened. No one can completely reassure you that everything will be all right when you are having bleeding and cramping. You know that it is abnormal, and it is appropriate for you to feel angry, hurt, depressed, and fearful. There is nothing *normal* about feeling pain, even though pain is commonplace.

I also had no idea of what to expect from the "baby" I was going to pass through my vagina. Would I see a whole baby, parts of one, or something very malformed? I know now that what you see also varies a lot from woman to woman, but it is never as scary as your imagination will lead you to expect.

What you do see is mostly blood—sometimes in large amounts—sometimes bright red, sometimes dark brownish or black. Often this blood is clotted and thick. As a general rule the more clotted material you pass, the more discomfort you will be feeling, although this is variable. If you have contractions, each one may force out clumps of clotted material.

Only rarely will you see fetal tissue that you can pick out as "baby" amidst the blood. Everything generally looks like large blood clots, although rarely you may see some lighter, almost tan-colored material mixed in. This material may appear fluffy if it is placental. This is tissue. The amount of tissue will depend on how long you have been pregnant. It may be golf ball-size if you abort at 10 weeks and larger for every week after. Sometimes the clots and tissue fragments come out all at once, or it may take several hours. Seeing recognizable tissue passed from you is generally less frightening than you would probably anticipate. As Ann, who had two miscarriages, described it:

> I had this morbid fear of seeing my baby—tiny but also distorted—in all the bloody mess that was coming out of me . . . and yet I couldn't see anything that really scared me, and it was all right that I looked.

Some women do see a formed infant, but again, this is not as frightening as one would think. A woman who had had a number of miscarriages told me this story:

It only lasted for a few minutes . . . very mild cramps
. . . and then it came out. It was a boy, I think. I was
sort of interested because it's amazing how formed it is
at only three to four months. It was small. I could look,
but it's awfully hard when it's your own, you really
want it.

Dr. Alice Rothchild deals with this by encouraging the
parents to see what is actually passed.

A miscarriage begins with the woman experiencing bleeding or cramping, and either one of these symptoms may
progress. Either the spot-bleeding increases or the cramping gets stronger. Finally she's passing either clots or
actual pieces of tissue. That's physically what she is
feeling.

But also she is probably terrified when this is happening, as most women are, and this is all happening
simultaneously with the physical symptoms. I think that
it is important for the mother to see what comes out. To
see that this is what came out of you, and this is it, and
it's ended. In fact, mothers who give birth at term to
congenitally malformed babies do better if they see the
baby. They don't focus on what was abnormal, but
what was normal. They see that it had ten fingers and
ten toes, and they feel reassured.

In that sense I think that it is good to save the
products of what comes out and say, "Look, see, this is
what came out of you, and it has ended." When you
can't see what is going on, it is much harder to accept
it.

This is how miscarriages happen—with bleeding, pain,
cramping, and a lot of emotional response. Sometime during
this you are dealing with your mate, your children, and the

entire medical establishment—your doctor and the hospital
staff. Your own feelings are altered and unfortunately sometimes heightened by their presence. Because of all these
variables each person's miscarriage experience is highly individual and slightly different.

You almost invariably have to deal with doctors and the rest
of the medical system. For me that was a very hard part of
having the miscarriage. I wanted a lot from my doctor. I also
knew well that the kind of attention I would receive would be
different if I were treated by hospital staff or other doctors.

There is, I have learned, as much variability in the warmth,
humanity, and understanding expressed by medical professionals as there is in the physical sensations of having a miscarriage.
Some people are cold and technical, and others are *right there*
when you need them with warmth and emotional support. The
trust I have placed in my obstetrician was well earned, but I
know other women whose experiences were not positive at all.
The whole environment of the hospital was as much part of the
miscarriage experience for me as the bleeding and cramping.

What you feel comes only in part from you; it also comes
from those around you. The love and support you get from
your mate, the rest of your family and your friends, and from
the medical personnel around you is extremely critical. We
depend on others to help us with our pain. When you feel that
you need to demand love and attention and answers from
those who are close to you and your doctor, you have every
right to do so.

SUMMARY

1. A miscarriage begins with bleeding and /or cramping. About one forth to one half of all pregnant
   women have some bleeding, but only half of them
   go on to miscarry.

2. The amount of bleeding and cramping that you have is not a certain indicator of your chances of having a miscarriage.

3. A miscarriage may be a long and painful ordeal, preceded by days of spotting, or it may occur very quickly.

4. The miscarriage will not affect your body or your reproductive future. You will probably be able to have as many normal children as you want.

5. What you actually see when you have the miscarriage is probably much less frightening than what you imagine.

6. If the bleeding stops and you carry your baby to term, it is as likely as any other baby to be completely normal.

IV

Conception
and Pregnancy

If you have had one or more spontaneous abortions, it is reasonable to wonder, "What does it take to make a normal child?" While we all know about the birds and the bees stuff from an early age, there is a lot more to having a baby than the act of sexual intercourse. Doing what comes naturally doesn't always result in a normal pregnancy, as you know if you have had to deal with a miscarriage.

That is because conception and pregnancy are very complex biological events. They require proper timing and the right biological environment. Any small mishap can prevent conception or terminate a pregnancy.

CONCEPTION

Anyone who has had a spontaneous abortion has conceived. That means that an egg and a sperm have united to form the beginning of a new life. From the single fertilized cell produced during conception the baby will grow. That cell is *totipotential*, which means that it contains all the biological information and potential biological structures necessary to make a complete human being.

Conception begins with an egg or ovum from the woman, and a sperm from the man. Eggs are produced by the mother's germ cells, located in the ovaries. These oval organs sit low in the abdomen, in the pelvis, where they are sheltered from accidents. Once a month usually one egg is fully matured and expelled from the ovary. Every woman is born with all the eggs that she will ever produce. These immature eggs lie dormant in the ovary and only one mature egg, which can be fertilized by a sperm, is produced each month. During the lifetime of the average woman about 400 eggs will mature and be made available for fertilization.

Men, however, are not born with a fixed number of sperm but instead produce them regularly in the testes, which are contained in the scrotum. While the testes and ovaries are really similar organs (they arise from the same origins in the developing fetus), they differ markedly in the way they produce germ cells. The testes are capable of producing an almost endless supply of sperm and expel millions of them during ejaculation.

For conception to occur, the production of normal eggs and normal sperm is essential. While there is always some possibility of error occurring later on in the pregnancy process, a good beginning is a prerequisite. Fortunately most couples who experience spontaneous abortions have normal ovaries and testes that produce normal eggs and sperm. Complicated tests of the hormone systems of the male and female partners are thus rarely helpful in determining the causes of recurrent spontaneous abortions. Some physicians do ask the male partner to have a sperm count and analysis, but finding an abnormality here is unlikely, since the couple was able to conceive.

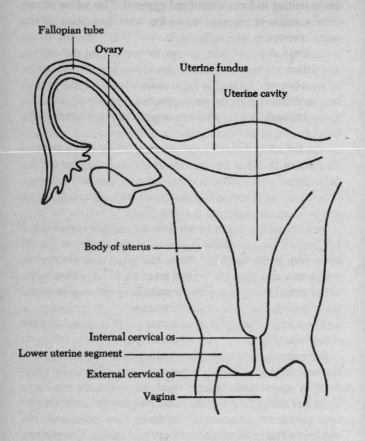

FIGURE 1   Female organs of reproduction

The actual process of conception depends on an egg and a sperm uniting to form a fertilized egg cell. This *union* occurs when a single sperm approaches the outer membrane of the ovum, pierces it at a right angle, and penetrates the ovum itself. Only one sperm will cross the membrane that covers the surface of the ovum. How the sperm pierces the membrane is not well understood, but once one sperm has pierced the membrane, all of the other sperm are repelled, presumably by immunological mechanisms which are activated within the egg.

How the sperm actually finds the egg depends on a complicated set of chemical interactions by which the sperm chemically "sees" the egg and is attracted to it. Some scientists still debate the existence of such a system of chemical affinities, yet it seems probable that it exists. These affinities are very complex and have yet to be worked out fully in humans, but it seems unlikely that the union of egg and sperm would occur only on a hit-or-miss basis. Further research is needed to give us a clearer picture of this set of chemical interactions.

The actual trip that the sperm make from the vagina to the egg is a long, arduous, and fascinating one.

If you look at Figure 1, a diagram of the woman's organs of reproduction, you can get an idea of the distance and route that the sperm must travel to meet with the egg. The sperm start out in the back of the vagina, having been deposited there by ejaculation during sexual intercourse. From there they enter the uterus through the os, or opening of the cervix. For most of the menstrual cycle the os remains closed, but during ovulation it relaxes and opens slightly. The sperm, aided by secretions from the glands that line the opening, enter the uterine cavity and make their way upward toward the egg. If these secretions are not present, the sperm cannot live or swim toward their goal, the ovum.

The ovaries, meanwhile, have produced one egg that is matured and expelled at the end of ovulation. It leaves the ovary and enters the Fallopian tube (see diagram), where fertilization eventually takes place. The exact mechanism by which the egg is expelled is also not completely understood. Fertilization, however, must take place in the Fallopian tube, so the expulsion of the egg from the ovary is an essential part of the conception process.

Unlike the sperm, the egg is not self-propelled, so it must be pushed out of the ovary and along the tube by tiny fibers that line the Fallopian tube and by rhythmic contractions of the tube itself. It is somewhere in the ampulla—a wider section of the tube where the walls are thinner—that fertilization takes place.

Meanwhile, the sperm are swimming upstream at a rapid pace. The entire distance is covered in about two or three hours. They swim at an extraordinary speed; the distance they travel is comparable to a journey of 150 miles for a human. All in all, very few sperm make it to the Fallopian tube, and only one sperm out of the 100 million or so that are ejaculated will fertilize the egg. The journey therefore must select the fastest and hardiest of sperm. In all probability this selection process is protective; it helps ensure that a healthy (and therefore probably normal) sperm will be involved in conception. Ultimately this will increase the likelihood of conceiving a normal child.

Let us emphasize that the couple who have had a miscarriage have been able to do all of this quite well. Remember that studies show that the couple who have had a miscarriage are at least as fertile as the general population. Some evidence indicates that they may even be slightly more fertile. Furthermore, they are able to conceive rather quickly after having a miscarriage.

PREGNANCY

Pregnancy is just as complex as conception, if not more so. Pregnancy involves the contributions of two living organisms— mother and child. It is here that we become sharply aware of the many factors that can affect the natural process and cause a spontaneous abortion. Not only does a normal pregnancy require that the biological environment (the mother's body) be adequate, but the embryo itself must be normal. If the embryo is not normal, then there is a very great likelihood that a miscarriage will occur.

The life of the new infant begins at the moment of fertilization, generally in the ampulla of the Fallopian tube. It is now that the process of *cleavage* begins. During cleavage the single cell that was formed by the union of sperm and egg duplicates itself and divides, forming two daughter cells. Cleavage continues in the Fallopian tube, producing a multicellular mass known as a *blastomere*. During this stage the cells remain undifferentiated. There is no way of knowing which cells will form the embryo itself, or the placenta, or any other part of the developing fetal system.

The final result of the cleavage process is a solid ball of cells called the *morula*. In the 72 hours that it takes for the morula to make its way to the uterus, there is intense biological activity. The cells duplicate and move continuously, reorienting themselves within the ball. By the time it enters the uterus, the morula contains approximately 12 cells, and the cells have begun to look different. In the few human samples studied to date, there has been one large centrally located cell, surrounded by 11 smaller ones.

Now two lines of cells begin to develop. One group, which grows more slowly, becomes the embryo. The other line will become the nourishing and protecting cells that help support the life of the fetus. This second group is called *trophoblastic* and is important because it is the origin of the placenta and other structures that are necessary to maintain intrauterine life.

On the fourth or fifth day of life the ball of cells becomes hollow and is now called a *blastocyst*. It is now about 60 cells residing in the uterus, and may be called a *conceptus*.

NIDATION

Growth of the conceptus cannot really begin until the blastocyst makes its way to the uterus. On or about the sixth day the blastocyst must find a home in the inner lining of the uterus. This "nesting" process, called *nidation*, takes a few days. Commonly the blastocyst will nest in the upper and rear portions of the uterus, finding for itself a secure and nourishing site in which to grow.

Nidation is an active physical and biochemical process that directly involves both the mother and the conceptus. First the ball of cells pierces the inner lining (endometrium) of the uterus and sinks into it. This lining has already been prepared to receive the conceptus by the hormones produced in the latter half of the menstrual cycle. In response to signals from both mother and conceptus this lining has been enriched and thickened. Once the blastocyst sinks into the endometrium, the lining heals over it and fastens it securely within uterus.

During these early days of life the conceptus begins to form a hollowed area. This fluid-filled hollow is formed by a membrane, the amnion, in which the fetus develops. In addition, at this stage of development the primary yolk sac seems to have the function of nourishing the trophoblast, even though some communication with the bloodstream of the mother probably exists as well.

At this stage the trophoblastic cells, which nourish and support the conceptus, still far outnumber the cells that make up the conceptus itself. Only later will the conceptus—by then called the embryo—begin to grow more rapidly. In other words first the connection with the mother is made secure. Then the structures that are destined to give support and nutrition must be developed before the body invests energy into the growth of the embryo.

If the morula fails to make its way from the Fallopian tube to the uterus, an abnormal pregnancy will result. This may cause an early spontaneous abortion or eventually may go on to be a tubal, or ectopic, pregnancy. If the conceptus is aborted early, the woman may only be aware of a late and rather heavy menstrual period. On the other hand a ruptured tubal pregnancy can cause severe hemorrhage, and even death if surgery cannot be performed in time to save the mother's life. Interestingly there have been cases in which nidation has occurred outside the tube or the uterus. Here the egg was probably fertilized in the tube, but growth has followed a slow rupture of the tube and continued in tissues other than the uterus or the Fallopian tube. Somehow the conceptus was able to make connections with the mother's blood supply in order to obtain nutrients. This is another example of the dynamic capabilities of the embryo. The conceptus will continue to grow until it is mechanically separated from the tissues it has nested upon.

Nidation, or nesting, is a two-way street. Signals from the mother and the conceptus interrelate to make a nest and provide suitable environment for growth. We are just beginning to unravel the complexities of this process, but suffice it to say that both partners (mother and fetus) must be normal for a normal pregnancy.

HORMONES

Hormones are the chemical substances that control all of these biological processes. They control the growth of the fetus and the environment that it grows in. They are produced by both the mother and the fetus—another aspect of the partnership that we have been describing. As in nidation, any alteration in the normal hormone balance can cause a spontaneous abortion.

At first all of the hormones come from the mother. Even before fertilization occurs, progesterone is produced to prepare the uterus to receive the fertilized egg. Progesterone comes from the *corpus luteum*, which is part of the ovary. This progesterone dominates the latter part of the menstrual cycle, after ovulation, so that the mother's body will be ready for nidation.

Among its many functions, progesterone acts to thicken and enrich the inner lining of the uterus. It also acts on the mammary glands and the placenta. It is clear now that progesterone is a very important hormone, and one about which there is still more to learn. For instance, it has recently been established that the corpus luteum is the major source of progesterone only in the early stages of pregnancy. After that, progesterone is produced in the placenta. We do not know what signals are involved in switching production from the corpus luteum to the placenta, but some signals must exist. This is another example of how the baby and the mother interact to make a normal pregnancy.

What happens if you do not produce enough progesterone? The conventional answer is that you will inevitably miscarry— and many studies have shown that this is true of women who have abnormally low levels of progesterone (found in the blood or urine). But the issue is less clear now that we know more about progesterone. It may be that a low progesterone level is an effect and not the cause of the problem. Perhaps it is only an indication of some other, more important problem?

An early answer to the problem of low progesterone was to give it, either by injection or vaginal suppository, to the pregnant woman. Since the results were often less than encouraging, doctors began to reevaluate the treatment. Either low progesterone production was not the problem or they were treating the wrong patients. In either case many turned away from its use. Moreover, there is some evidence that progesterone (especially the synthetic forms) can cause birth defects in the limbs or heart of an otherwise normal infant. Thus, treating the effect and not the cause could be dangerous as well as fruitless.

One gynecologist/obstetrician who continues to treat his patients with progesterone believes that the risk is negligible:

> Progesterone is one of the harmless hormones, so if the patient shows poor progesterone secretion and poor maturation of the endometrium (inner lining of the uterus) I treat her. We do this by giving the progesterone after she ovulates as indicated by her temperature graph, even before we know that she is pregnant. The vaginal suppository is very easy for the patient to use, and that is what we give.

The opposing view is becoming more prevalent, however. We do not know that a low progesterone level is the cause of spontaneous abortions, and we do know that by giving progesterone one might damage an otherwise normal infant. Here is an explanation by an obstetrician who does not use progesterone to treat his patients who miscarry:

> Human pregnancy appears to be corpus-luteum dependent [progesterone comes from the corpus luteum] for the

first four weeks, but after that it is unclear what it is that maintains it.

Patients who abort tend to have their progesterone levels fall, probably because they are aborting. The cause-and-effect relationship is not what people originally thought it was. It is probably not the hormonal problem that is the etiology of the abortion. There is also great controversy whether there is useful treatment. Some studies suggest that it may be a useful treatment, but I am very reluctant to treat people with it. . . . We just don't know what we are treating, and there is some small danger in the treatment itself.

Although the controversy still goes on, neither the drug manufacturers nor the FDA approve of using progesterone in such cases, and this is no longer generally accepted medical practice.

Some obstetricians give human chorionic gonadotropin (HCG) or Clomid® in an attempt to stimulate ovulation, and thus the mother's production of progesterone. HCG is a hormone produced by the trophoblast early in pregnancy. It is necessary in maintaining a normal pregnancy and in fact when you go in for a pregnancy test, you are actually being tested for the presence of HCG. Unfortunately there are not any reliable studies on the effects of HCG in preserving pregnancy, and its use may involve similar risks, since the mother's body will produce additional amounts of progesterone.

Again, we are dealing with a cause-and-effect problem. The falling progesterone level may be the effect of an abnormal conceptus, and not a deficiency in the mother's ability to produce this hormone. Giving HCG or progesterone would then only treat the effect and have no beneficial role in dealing with the underlying problem. In such a case, when our scientific understanding is still limited, you must decide for yourself what treatments are advisable. One thing that is certain, though, is that all of these hormones can have side effects of their own.

A BIOLOGICAL PERSPECTIVE

Your ability to make appropriate decisions about your health care will depend to a large extent on your understanding of the biology of reproduction and your acceptance of the fact that in this area much is not known. Often drugs like diethylstilbestrol (DES) and thalidomide have been administered without an adequate understanding of their potential effects— and often with tragic results.

Unfortunately for the parents who have had recurrent spontaneous abortions, this lack of scientific knowledge is extremely frustrating. There is a tendency for these parents, who want very much to have children, to accept treatments that may not be helpful and sometimes are quite dangerous. It is important to proceed cautiously, with an ever-present awareness that intervening in the normal process of reproduction always carries some risk—and that as yet we have not found an absolutely safe and reliable means of averting a threatened miscarriage.

In the normal biological process of reproduction nidation does not always take place. In cases of lethal or severe abnormalities in the embryo, nidation may not take place for good reason. We have tried to describe the complexity of nesting to help you realize how many factors must be at work if the blastocyst is to find a secure home in the uterine endometrium. We must accept that nature is more concerned with the survival of the species than with each individual conception. Thus, some fish must lay millions of eggs to ensure that just a few will hatch, and we should expect that not every conceptus that is formed will develop into a full-term infant.

Thus you must be patient, both with the biological complexity of pregnancy and with the present lack of good medical treatment for the problem of repeated spontaneous abortions. However, most couples who have had recurrent miscarriages will eventually have a successful pregnancy if they continue to try—and they can do this without taking any drugs to support the pregnancy.

SUMMARY

1. Conception and pregnancy are very complex biological events that require a normal egg from the mother and a normal sperm from the father.
2. Anyone who has had a miscarriage has been able to conceive and is actually fertile. Some studies show that couples who miscarry are more fertile than the average.
3. Fusion of an egg and sperm in the Fallopian tube begins the pregnancy. This is called fertilization.
4. The fertilized egg grows by dividing, then makes its way to the uterus, where it nests (nidation) and begins to receive nourishment from the mother.
5. Hormones are chemicals that regulate the pregnancy process. These hormones come from both the mother and the fetus. Any imbalance or deficiency in these hormones can trigger a spontaneous abortion.
6. Giving these hormones by mouth, injection, or vaginal suppository is medically controversial. No one knows whether these hormones can save a pregnancy, and there is some evidence that they

can cause abnormalities in an otherwise normal infant. To date the drug companies and the government have not approved progesterone or other hormones for the maintenance of pregnancy.

V

Genetic Causes of Miscarriage

From the very beginning I wanted to know why I was aborting. But as I asked more questions about reproduction and genetics I had more questions than the medical community had answers. The theory that a spontaneous abortion is actually the body's natural way of rejecting an abnormal pregnancy seemed overly simplified. It helped me to deal with my guilt feelings, but the haziness of this basic scientific understanding left me feeling uncertain.

The theory states that a spontaneous abortion is nature's way of protecting humankind from the consequences of the mistakes that are sometimes made at conception. It maintains that since conception is very complicated, mistakes do occasionally happen. Since small mistakes can cause serious abnormalities, it is the job of the woman's body to keep mankind from perpetuating these mistakes.

This theory did not give me a *cure* for my problem. There was no drug that I could take or treatment that I could have that would give me a normal pregnancy. I learned to have some degree of hope, but only after many people told me about their miscarriages and subsequent normal pregnancies.

After a while I did accept what I had learned, and it did help me to face the future. As I understood more about the science of genetics I realized that most of these errors or abnormalities are caused by random events during the very early stages of reproduction. However, this did not explain why I had had three miscarriages and other people had none.

There has been some research in the field of immunology that may someday help to explain this question. Except for the rare couple who are found to carry a genetic error that they are passing on to their offspring, we usually do not find out why we have repeated miscarriages. So for most couples, as for Mark and me, the miscarriage problem remains largely unexplained.

Whatever the cause, miscarriages are devastating emotionally and physically. Even if they are not actually caused by genetic errors all of the time, I am now convinced that this is the case much of the time. Fortunately most of these errors seem to be caused by random accidents that affect the parents' sex cells. Though there is no way of preventing this from happening, sooner or later chance will favor you and you will be successful in having a baby. Before I could accept this and receive some hope from it, I had to learn about heredity.

BASIC HEREDITY

Let us start from conception, the beginning of a new life. As we discussed in Chapter 4, it takes an egg from the mother and a sperm from the father to make a baby. Half of what we are comes from each parent, and each half is transmitted to the baby by the genetic material in the ovum and sperm.

This basic genetic material which conveys all the information for what we are is the *gene*. It is so basic that the science of genetics is named for this fundamental structure. Genes are very small units of chemicals that are found in the center, or nucleus, of each cell in our body. The nucleus occupies the center of the cell the way the yolk sits in the center of a fried egg.

Genes are the storehouse of information that control all life. What your body will turn out to be, biologically at least, is determined by these chemicals. Each parent provides half of the baby's characteristics through these chemicals. Try to think of the genes as bits of information stored in a living computer. This information is used by the computer to carry out all of its tasks. In the cell it is the "brain" that originates all activity, and without it there would be no life function.

Genes do not float around loosely in the cell. They are wrapped up together on long strands of sticky material into structures called *chromosomes*. Each chromosome is made up of many genes, and it is the chromosome that we study when we look for abnormalities in the heredity of the fetus. In all, there are 46 chromosomes in the normal human cell.

During the process of cell division the chromosomes pair up, making 23 pairs. Thus when the cell is studied for errors (and it is studied during the division process) it is these pairs that are analyzed. Figure 2 is a simplified picture of a cell with the chromosomes in the nucleus. At this point (metaphase) they are paired but spread out randomly in the nucleus.

If these chromosomes are defective, an abnormality occurs that will cause a problem with the embryo. Any defect is usually disastrous. It kills the embryo or at least causes a major disruption in the normal growth process. Currently it is theorized that when the mother's body recognizes this abnormality the rejection process is activated. Then a spontaneous abortion occurs.

The abnormal chromosomes that cause this rejection can

come from one of two sources—the parents or the embryo. Most of the time it seems that the abnormality comes from the ovum or sperm of the parents. Further, it is thought that the occurrence of these chromosomal defects is largely random. Remember that a large percentage of all spontaneous abortions are thought to be caused by chromosomal defects; 95 percent of these chromosomal defects are caused by purely chance events. Some ova and sperm just seem to have defects. Biology is not perfect.

However, sometimes these errors are part of the regular make-up of the parents' ova and sperm. These defects can be uncovered by genetic testing. It is important for parents to know whether they have such chromosomal errors, because they may be passing them on to their children at the time of conception. We will discuss this in more detail later in this chapter, but the main point is that parents can *transmit* errors in chromosomes to their children through permanent defects in their own ova and sperm. Such errors are called *translocations*.

The error, however, can originate in the embryo. In these cases, the problem has nothing to do with the parents' ovum or sperm, but occurs as a *de novo* (completely new) event very early in the life of the embryo. Sometimes this error happens as a random event during early growth, while at other times chemicals, infections, drugs and radiation may be the cause. Later on in this chapter we will list some of the more common drugs and chemicals that can cause chromosomal errors, and in Chapter 10 we will discuss the role of infections in this problem.

To understand fully how these two events happen—the transmission of genetic errors from the parents and the creation of entirely new ones in the fetus—we must first learn how cells grow. It is during this growing process, when cells are dividing and their chromosomes are reproducing themselves, that these genetic mistakes occur.

HOW CELLS GROW

When a cell makes a duplicate of itself (like a carbon copy), growth occurs. One cell becomes two, two become four, four become eight, and so on, until millions and millions of cells are formed, making up the mature human body. To accomplish this growth, the chromosomes in the nucleus of each cell must copy themselves. If they did not do so, the nucleus of the new cell would not have the genetic information necessary to carry out the life processes. This process of cell division is called *mitosis*.

Figure 3 is a simplified picture of a cell, with two pairs of chromosomes (not 23 pairs, as is normal) undergoing mitosis. At first each chromosome makes a copy of itself, in Step 2. This is called *replication*.

At this point the chromosomes are still very long, thin, dispersed strands. They now shorten by coiling up. As they shorten they concentrate and can be seen under the miscroscope if they are stained with special dyes. When the strands can be seen, the cell is in a stage of mitosis called prophase. Next, in metaphase, the chromosomes can be seen as paired forms, as in our schematic representation in Step 2.

In Step 3 the chromosomes separate into two sets, each one destined for a separate new cell. This stage is called anaphase. The chromosomes at this stage move to opposite regions of the cell, readying themselves to become part of an entirely new cell. In Step 4 the process is complete, and two new, identical cells have been produced.

This process, although simplified in this diagram, is what goes on in the embryo just after conception. The original cell produced by the fusion of the parents' ovum and sperm divides to produce new cells that will eventually make up the entire infant.

Any error in this process of mitosis, especially during the very early stages of life immediately after conception, can

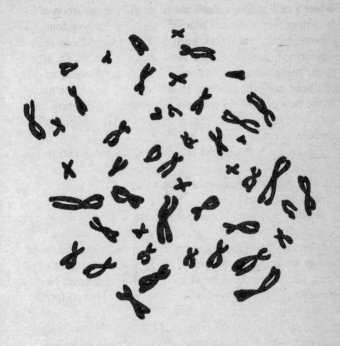

FIGURE 2 Stained chromosomes in a normal human cell

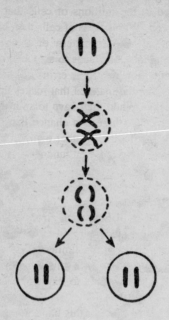

FIGURE 3   Mitosis

cause a major abnormality in the fetus. Errors that occur in the embryonic stage are not easily tolerated, since the original error is multiplied in the millions of cells that grow from a defective parent cell. Whole lines of cells then become abnormal and the normal growth pattern of the fetus becomes disorganized. Eventually this leads to a spontaneous abortion.

The exact manner in which these errors occur is not known. What is known is that the material that makes up the chromosomes is very sticky. When they have to split up and go into different daughter cells, there is a chance that some sections of different strands will stick together inappropriately. If they do not divide into exactly the right numbers, one cell may get 47 chromosomes while the other cell will have only 45 chromosomes. In either case an abnormal fetus will have been produced.

The "sticky" theory of how such errors originate is obviously an imprecise one, since our understanding of the factors that control mitosis is still very limited. It is natural to feel some amount of frustration with this scientific vagueness, especially if it is all you have to explain your miscarriage problem.

Clearly the earlier in life that this happens, the more likely it is to be deadly to the developing embryo. A well advanced fetus with millions and millions of cells is better able to survive an error in the growth of a cell than an embryo in the blastocyst stage, for instance. The more developed organism has many normal cells to fall back on. However, the primitive embryonic form that is composed of just a few cells is critically in need of each one to function and divide normally.

The probability is that most genetic errors do not come about in this way. Most come from a defective ovum, and/or sperm, that originates in the parents. To understand this, we need to learn about *meiosis,* the process by which ova and sperm are produced. Meiosis is similar to mitosis, except that the number of chromosomes is halved. Each normal egg or sperm has 23 chromosomes, not 46, since in meiosis the cells go through an added stage of division.

Figure 4 is a simplified scheme of meiosis. In meiosis the first few steps (in this diagram Steps 1–4) are very much like mitosis. The chromosomes make duplicates of themselves, and two daughter cells are produced that are identical to the parent cell. However, as the process continues the pairs of chromosomes themselves split up. When the pairs split, the number of chromosomes in each daughter cell is reduced by half. Four cells are produced, and each has 23 chromosomes, not 46.

This is the biological process of both ova and sperm production that goes on in the ovaries and testes. These sex cells have half the number of chromosomes so that when conception occurs, it will produce an embryo with the normal amount of genetic material. Two halves make a whole, and life continues as we know it. If it did not happen this way, the embryo would have 92 chromosomes and be abnormal. If one person with 92 chromosomes mated with another, a baby with 184 chromosomes would be born, and so on and so on indefinitely. Life could not continue as we know it without the process of meiosis.

But *because of this halving process, errors can occur during meiosis.* As we said earlier in our discussion of mitosis, chromosomes are long strands of very sticky material. This means that pieces of chromosomes or whole chromosomes often stick to each other in inappropriate ways. Thus, back in Figure 4, it is possible that Cell A might receive a chromosome meant for Cell B. If this were to occur, Cell B would lack a chromosome and Cell A would have an extra one. Both cells would be abnormal.

This can take place either in the ova or the sperm. There is some evidence that most of the chromosomal errors that produce spontaneous abortions originate in the number of chromosomes in the ovum. This observation points to the notion that sperm with the wrong number of chromosomes may not be as capable of fertilization as normal sperm are.

However, it is known that both sperm and ova can undergo these meiotic errors, and so both the mother's and the father's sex cells may cause the problem.

In Figure 5 we have drawn a picture of the kind of abnormal meiosis that we have described. In the drawing we have taken out the other 21 chromosomes to make the picture a bit simpler. What is important to realize is that between Steps 4 and 5, Cell A loses a chromosome and Cell B mistakenly picks it up. If these were human ova or sperm, one cell would have 22 chromosomes while the other would have 24. Both cells contain a genetic error.

Sometimes only parts of chromosomes are lost or gained during meiosis. In these cases the new daughter cell (be it ovum or sperm) may have 45½ or 46½ chromosomes. When part of one chromosome is found attached to another, this is called a *translocation*. In either case a mismatch in the number of chromosomes or their rearrangement is likely to be lethal to the child.

In general we need all of the information stored in our genes for normal growth. Our genes have been selected over thousands of years of mating to produce an exceedingly complex system in which all of the parts are integrated. Small mistakes on the genetic level are really big mistakes for the entire organism. Thus the loss of any part of a chromosome can cause a growth abnormality. Theoretically this will be recognized by the mother's body and rejected by means of a spontaneous abortion.

Sometimes abnormal infants are born. In these cases, for instance Down's syndrome (mongolism), children are born with an extra chromosome and do survive. In theory this represents a failure of the miscarriage process, but we can tolerate an extra chromosome a little better than a missing one, even though this creates a serious abnormality.

There are many examples of both kinds of problem—additions and deletions of chromosomes. Down's syndrome is probably the best known of the additions. These intellectually retarded children have a condition called *trisomy*. In this condition the added chromosome is commonly attached to the twenty-first chromosome and is called Trisomy 21. The addition can also be found on chromosome 13 or 18.

Additions of sex chromosomes (X, Y in Figure 6, pair 23) are also possible, as in Klinefelter's syndrome, in which an extra X chromosome is present (XXY instead of the normal XY). Children who are born with an extra X chromosome will be sterile and they may exhibit a wide range of normal and abnormal male physical characteristics. An XXX condition also exists, as does an XYY. It is necessary to have at least one X chromosome to survive. Children born with only one X chromosome (Turner's syndrome) will be unable to produce normal sex hormones and will have other physical abnormalities. You can see from this that the proper distribution of chromosomes during meiosis is essential.

"BAD-LUCK GENES"

Our current knowledge of cellular genetics leads us to believe that the majority of the errors during meiosis happen purely by chance. In other words, given the millions of sperm that are produced and the hundreds of ova that are matured, some errors in the process are inevitable. When these errors cause a spontaneous abortion it is "bad luck" and not something that you as parents could control.

However, there are some factors that influence the frequency with which these errors can occur, and there is sometimes more than just luck involved. We spoke earlier in Chapter 2 of the role of age in causing spontaneous abortions. As the couple gets older there is more likely to be a chromosomal error. You cannot change your age, but if you are over 35 you still stand a very good chance of having a normal baby.

There are factors that you can control. *Teratogens* are agents that cause developmental defects in the embryo or the fetus. In the laboratory and in human studies a number of drugs and chemicals have been shown to have an impact on fetal development. They include hormones (including the oral contraceptive, or birth-control pill), plastics, petroleum products, radiation, anesthetics, alcohol, caffeine, tobacco, and many other substances.

The role of these agents in causing spontaneous abortions is not yet well understood. The focus of most research in both humans and animals has been on genetic defects that only become apparent at birth. But, we do know that some agents that cause growth disturbances in the embryo may be capable of precipitating a miscarriage. It might be prudent for couples who have experienced repeated spontaneous abortions to avoid contact with suspected teratogens.

What follows is a list of some of these agents. This is only a partial list, and we must learn more about how these substances influence spontaneous abortions. Studies of the relationship between narcotics use and spontaneous abortion have already demonstrated how serious this problem can be. In one such study the miscarriage rates of two groups of women—narcotics users and nonusers—were compared. Although both groups' miscarriage rates were less than 15 percent, the narcotics users as a group had almost twice as many miscarriages (10.2 versus 5.8 percent).

It must be remembered, however, that drug abusers often have poor nutritional habits and other problems that might increase their risk of aborting. Further research is important in this area.

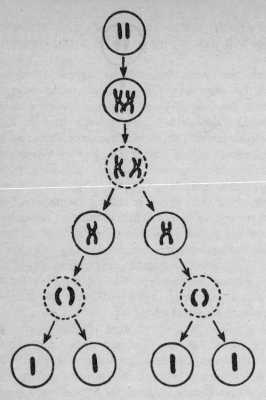

FIGURE 4   Meiosis

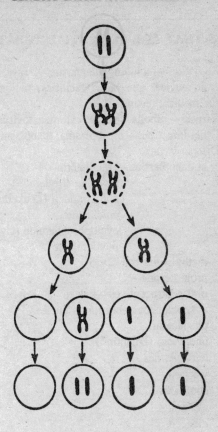

FIGURE 5   Abnormal meiosis

AGENTS THAT ARE POTENTIAL TERATOGENS

1. Radiation—including diagnostic X rays, emissions from nuclear generating facilities, radioactive dyes for medical testing
2. Viruses—rubella, herpes, cytomegalovirus
3. Other infections—mycoplasma, toxoplasma, brucella
4. Drugs
   antineoplastics—aminopterin
                   busulfan (Myleran®)
                   chlorambucil (Leukeran®)
                   colchicine
                   cyclophosphamide (Cytoxan®)
                   methotrexate
   diethylstilbestrol (DES)
   progesterone
   oral contraceptives—link to
      spontaneous abortion is unclear
   phenacetin
   phenytoin (Dilantin®)
   tetracyclines
   warfarin
   coumarin
   alcohol
   tobacco
   streptomycin
   lithium
   narcotics (morphine, heroin, etc.)
   reserpine
   vitamin D (in massive doses)
   chlordiazepoxide (Librium®)—under investigation
   diazepam (Valium®)—under investigation
   anesthetics—under investigation

A very important factor that must be considered is the time during your pregnancy that you take these drugs. It is currently felt that the greatest danger lies between day 20 and day 90 of pregnancy. It is during this time that the major organ systems for the baby are forming. Thus most of the children born with defects are thought to have been critically affected during this developmental period.

However, we cannot be certain that defects that lead to spontaneous abortions do not happen earlier in the pregnancy process. Therefore we should assume that any potentially damaging drug or agent should also be avoided during the first 20 days of embryonic life—and in practice even for a period of time before that, just as you would stop taking an oral contraceptive some time before you attempt to become pregnant, even though the potential danger to the embryo has not been proved. Certainly this is wise if you have had problems with repeated spontaneous abortions.

One obstetrician we interviewed put it this way:

> We really don't know what causes these genetic defects. What we do know is that the reproductive system is a sensitive one, and that many chemicals and drugs can affect it. If a couple has had one or more spontaneous abortions, I encourage them to avoid all sorts of agents when they are trying to get pregnant. This is only good common sense.
>
> This applies to drugs they take while they are trying to get pregnant. If they need the drug as a life-sustaining thing, well, then it is understandable. But if it isn't completely necessary, or if they can change their work environment for the time they are trying to get pregnant, that is all advisable.
>
> I also tell them that all of this is unproven, and that their problem may very well be just due to chance. But since I can't assure them that it isn't, it is wise to be cautious.

We are becoming increasingly aware of the role of our environment in all kinds of health issues, and we hope that future research will document the effect of teratogens on spontaneous abortions. We just do not know as yet how the spraying of pesticides, the dumping of chemicals that eventually seep into our water supply, and the waste emitted by nuclear power plants affect the incidence of miscarriages. Not enough research has been done on this subject yet. We do know, for instance, that more birth defects were reported in Hiroshima after the population was exposed to radiation, but no reliable studies on the rate of miscarriage are available. It would seem worthwhile to devote more attention to this area, so that we can better understand the role of our environment in causing pregnancy loss.

BALANCED TRANSLOCATIONS

While the errors in chromosomes that we have been talking about until now have been due to chance ("bad-luck genes"), a balanced translocation is part of the permanent genetic structure of one or both of the parents. For these parents a miscarriage is not merely bad luck but the product of the transmission of this translocation to their children.

A translocation means a rearrangement of the chromosomal material. A piece of one chromosome is tacked onto another chromosome, not its normally paired partner, and stays there. It is reproduced in this way when the cell duplicates its chromosomes during meiosis. When this happens an egg or sperm is produced that has an abnormal chromosomal pattern. Some but not all of these translocations are deadly to the embryo and can cause a spontaneous abortion.

To get a better idea of a translocation, look at Figure 6. In this picture we have two pairs of chromosomes, one with letters signifying the genes and the other with numbers. We will use this example to show you how a translocation works; here a piece of the numbered chromosome will be added on to the lettered one.

Look at chromosome number 4. To the left of the arrow this chromosome has genes numbered one through nine. During meiosis (depicted by the arrow) a piece of chromosome number 4 (with genes 8 and 9) is lost to chromosome number one. Why this happens is not completely understood, but it may have to do with the stickiness of the chromosome material. When chromosome number 1 gets genes 8 and 9 from chromosome number 4, a translocation occurs. Now both chromosomes, number 1 and number 4, are abnormal. If an ovum containing either of these chromosomes is fertilized, a genetic abnormality will be produced. Parents who carry these translocations are always at greater risk of having a miscarriage.

Your physician is likely to use the term *balanced translocation*. This means that the total amount of chromosomal material stays the same in the cell. Thus, in the individual cell there is no net gain or loss of chromosomal material, but an incorrect rearrangement. The total amount of genetic material is constant, but the information in the genetic code may be dramatically altered. The code is read along the chromosome in linear fashion. The order of the information is just as important as the content. So a rearrangement of the order may be as lethal to the developing embryo as the addition or deletion of a chromosome.

Even if you carry a translocation, it does not mean that you are destined to have abnormal children or endless miscarriages. You do need good genetic counseling, because every translocation acts differently during reproduction.

Figuring out the chances of having a spontaneous abortion with a given translocation is not always easy. This is because there are few scientific studies of the probability of a given translocation's causing a miscarriage. But a genetic counselor

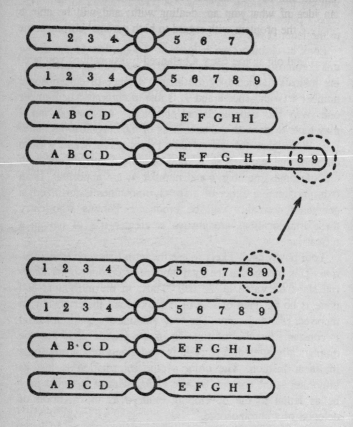

FIGURE 6   Producing a translocation

should still be very helpful for you. He or she can give you an idea of what you are dealing with, and will be able to analyze the problem with regard to both parents' chromosome structure.

To find out if you carry a balanced translocation, you need to have your chromosomes tested. This involves a simple blood test, using a sample taken from a vein. After the blood is drawn, some of the cells (lymphocytes) will be specially stained and examined under a microscope. A picture of the chromosomes inside the nucleus of the cell will be made. This is called an *idiogram*, or *karyotype*. It can then be analyzed for errors in the normal number, size, and arrangement of the chromosomal material. It can tell you if you carry a translocation that you may be passing on to your child. Figure 7 is an example of a normal male karyotype.

Even if you do have such a translocation, you can still have normal children. Some authorities estimate that there is only a 5 percent chance of a translocation's causing repeated spontaneous abortions, yet this figure is not exact. What you will learn from genetic testing is whether or not you are carriers of a translocation. If it turns out that you are, you can have amniocentesis to check the fetus once you do become pregnant. This information should make you feel optimistic, not pessimistic.

The cost of chromosomal analysis is generally around $300 for each parent. It is provided free by some centers that have received grants to study genetic abnormalities. Considering the cost of other medical tests that you may be asked to go through, it is probably very worthwhile to do this. Also, since genetic testing merely requires a simple blood test, it involves little danger or pain.

When should you have this genetic testing? The answer is less clear now than it was a few years ago, when it was rarely done. It used to be thought that genetic testing of both parents' chromosomes was useful only after three consecutive

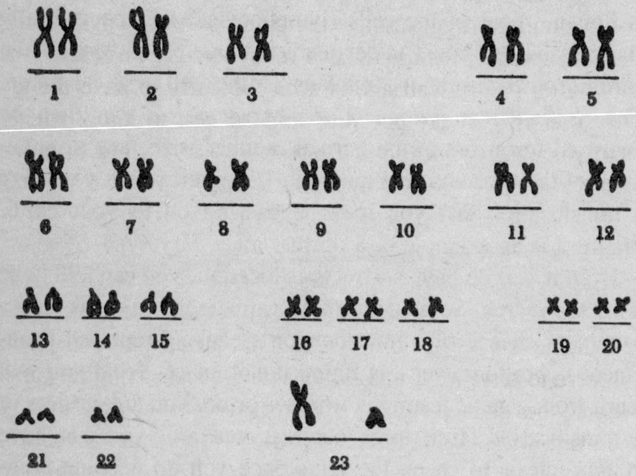

FIGURE 63 Karyotype of normal male chromosome arrangement

spontaneous abortions. That was because most centers were not able to perform the test, and it was known that most spontaneous abortions are caused by chance events. But now many doctors—especially those with an interest in genetics—will perform the test after two miscarriages.

We think that the decision to have genetic testing rests with the parents. It is as much an emotional issue as a medical one. You may want to have the chromosome analysis after a second spontaneous abortion to relieve your own fears. Probably after one miscarriage is a bit too early to have the test, but after two it may put your mind at rest to know whether you carry a translocation. If you have had a child born with an abnormality, *and* a spontaneous abortion, it is probably also wise to have your chromosomes analyzed.

If you ask for chromosome testing, your doctor should consent. The procedure is a relatively harmless one, and the results are likely to make you and your mate feel better. Medicine is a service profession. That means that your doctor is there to serve you, and reasonable requests from the patient should be granted. Even if he or she would not normally proceed with testing after two miscarriages, it is probably advisable to do so if the parents are anxious about this. Dr. Marylou Buyse, a genetic counselor, explained this.

> If the parents want a test, they should insist on it. Many obstetricians will say that they don't need it, but that they will send them for it if they really want. The doctor says, Go try again to have a baby.
>
> I think that these parents would benefit from knowing whether they are carrying a genetic abnormality that may be transmitted to the fetus. They can have some reassurance if they find out that they don't carry an abnormality, and if they carry one, they should know it and have the information to make a reasonable choice about it.

AMNIOCENTESIS

Amniocentesis is a procedure for testing the chromosomes of the fetus during the fourth month of pregnancy. This provides the parents with the opportunity to terminate an abnormal pregnancy voluntarily. It is indicated if you have had a genetically abnormal child before, if you know that one or both of you carry a translocation, or if you have had repeated spontaneous abortions and are concerned about the normality of your baby. It is commonly recommended for women over 35.

Amniocentesis can determine if the fetus has any of several potential problems, including neural tube defects, enzymatic deficiencies, and Rh disease. Later in pregnancy amniocentesis can give information about the level of maturation of the fetus's lungs. It involves obtaining a sample of fluid from the amniotic cavity in which the fetus floats. This fluid contains cells that are shed by the fetus during its life in the uterus. These cells are obtained in or about the fourteenth to sixteenth week of pregnancy, when the fluid is abundant, the infant small enough to allow room for the needle puncture, and there is a chance to repeat the test if the tap is unsuccessful or the fluid cannot be cultured. The procedure can be performed before this but at an increased risk.

Many physicians recommend that all women over 35 have the test, even if they have a normal obstetric history. We do know that the incidence of genetic abnormalities goes up as women grow older, but this may or may not be sufficient reason to use the test as a screening procedure. In our earlier discussion of how chromosomes act during cell division, we tried to emphasize that more errors occur as we age. Thus, 1 birth in 2000 will be abnormal for women of 20 while 1 in 32 will be abnormal (e.g., Down's syndrome) for women of 45. It is not that the chromosomes change (although research into this is going on), but more mistakes occur in their distribution during cell division.

To perform the amniocentesis, local anesthesia is used, and you are awake and in a reclining position on your back. After you have emptied your bladder, the person performing the test will palpate your uterus and decide where to insert the needle. In many centers ultrasound will be used to establish the position of the fetal structures more exactly.

After the abdomen is washed and painted with sterilizing solution, the anesthetic (like Novocain used by the dentist) will be injected under the skin. A fine (19–22 gauge spinal-type) needle is inserted into the amniotic cavity, and 10–15 ml of amniotic fluid is removed. The fluid is then sent to a laboratory for culturing and analysis. As with any medical procedure, amniocentesis has its risks. It is possible to introduce infection when the needle is inserted. Further, traumatic injury to either the mother or the fetus can occur. This may mean rupturing the membranes, sensitizing the mother to the Rh factor, or directly injuring either the fetus or the placenta with the needle.

For our purposes the most important danger is that of inducing a spontaneous abortion. Estimates of the frequency of this range from 2 to 5 percent. The figures depend somewhat on the training and ability of the person performing the procedure and the number of times the needle has to be inserted before the fluid is obtained. Some authorities say that the use of ultrasound can reduce the risk as well.

It is difficult to evaluate the significance of this 2 to 5 percent risk factor since we do not have reliable data on the frequency of second-trimester spontaneous abortions in general. They appear to be very rare; the rate is variously estimated at 1 to 2 or 3 percent. There is also some evidence that this figure goes up slightly for women over 35—who are also more likely to undergo amniocentesis. Thus the risk that amniocentesis involves is only slightly greater (if at all) than the ordinary risk of spontaneous abortion in the second trimester.

Since the procedure is performed after the fourteenth week of pregnancy and since it takes three or more weeks to obtain the results, you will have to have a saline and/or prostaglandin abortion if you decide to voluntarily terminate your pregnancy. This involves inducing labor by injecting one (or possibly both) of these substances into the amniotic cavity. This procedure and the subsequent labor is considerably more painful and emotionally distressing than the suction or curettage abortions performed during the first trimester.

As with any procedure you, the patient, must decide whether the risks outweigh the rewards. If you have had repeated spontaneous abortions, and you know that you or your partner carries a genetic abnormality, the procedure may help you reassure yourself that your child will be normal. If you are older, you will have to consider the increased risk of genetic defects. You should not undergo amniocentesis unless you are willing to consider an induced abortion. There is no point in risking danger to yourself or the pregnancy if you are morally opposed to elective abortions.

EMOTIONAL ADJUSTMENTS
TO GENETIC ISSUES

When you begin to think about genetics, it can be a frightening issue. If one or both of you have a genetic translocation, it may make you feel angry and helpless. There is no cure for a translocation, and this can be emotionally crushing when you first hear about it.

What you need to remind yourself is that the effects of every translocation are different. Most of them will not prevent you from having as many normal children as you want. That is why genetic testing should be accompanied by genetic counseling. You need to know exactly what the nature of your problem is and its likely effects on your reproductive future. A good genetic counselor is a must in this regard.

Even with good counseling you should expect to feel guilty, ashamed, resentful, and angry if you find out that you are carrying a genetic abnormality. It is normal, and productive, to feel angry and frustrated because one or both of you carry a translocation. Anger can release tensions, but remember that *it is the translocation and not the person that is the enemy*. The person has not changed; only your knowledge that he or she has a genetic problem is new.

There is also the danger that you may use the medical problem as a smoke screen to cover other emotional problems that may be occurring in the relationship. If you have other disappointments, points of disagreement, or old wounds in the relationship, it is all too easy to use the medical problem as the catch-all subject to fight about. That will not help you adjust to your miscarriage.

When talking with each other, attempt to stick to the point and be honest about what you feel. If you are angry about financial problems, sexual difficulties, or other family problems, try to avoid using the genetic issue as a weapon to hurt the other person. Keep the issues as clear and as separate as possible. And if you run into snags, be open. If you get to points that can't be resolved, try enlisting the help of a person who is trained in family counseling.

Once you understand the genetic problem, go back and try to discuss your reproductive future in the light of your new knowledge. For most couples a translocation does not mean that they cannot have normal children. It may be a bit harder than it is for the average couple yet still a likely reality.

Dr. Buyse had some important words to say about the emotional issues that come out of reproductive genetic testing:

> One of the universal feelings that the couple has, whether
> they have a spontaneous abortion or a child with a

genetic problem, is guilt. When one of them is identified as responsible, the other party has a normal tendency to blame. In that sense that makes the guilt even stronger.

I think that for most couples who have a mutually supportive relationship guilt is an unacceptable feeling. If you wanted to have a child and you find out that your wife has a translocation and your choices are miscarriage, worrying about the pregnancy and amniocentesis, or adoption—there is room to feel a certain resentment. *That's okay. It doesn't mean that you resent your partner, just the situation.*

Also, if there is some marital discord—and the incidence of that is very high, as we know—this kind of issue can feed into that. People are very sensitive about their reproductive capacity. This is a society where on many levels the inability to reproduce is a reflection on your manhood or your womanhood. Even if they don't think that way, they express it on some level.

In a relationship where you love someone and you feel very close, there is a certain inhibition against expressing all this. It is not an acceptable thing to say, but it is something that on some level needs to be said.

I think that it can be said in a supportive way. I think that you can say, ''Gee, I really hate the situation. I am very angry and resentful about it.'' It doesn't mean that you are necessarily angry with the person at all. That is the distinction. It is the situation and not the person.

CHROMOSOME ANALYSIS OF THE ABORTED FETUS

Until recently researchers have been very much involved in studying the genetics of the aborted fetus. This was done to learn more about miscarriages and to prove or reject the hypothesis that most spontaneous abortions are actually caused by genetic defects. This scientific research was essential to our current understanding.

Now that the genetic theory of miscarriage has been accepted in medicine, chromosomal testing of the infant is less important. Moreover it is somewhat difficult to perform the test. To study the chromosomes of the aborted fetus (abortus), cells must be grown in the laboratory. This depends on getting fresh, uncontaminated specimens. Viral contamination, common in the aborted tissue, will prevent successful culturing.

Getting the specimens is also not easy. Unless the miscarriage happens fairly late in pregnancy, the woman cannot always see the tissue and know what to save. If the woman is having her first miscarriage, she is not likely to know enough to save the tissue. And for many women it is emotionally unpleasant to have to do this.

Since we already know that approximately 50 percent of first-trimester spontaneous abortions are caused by genetic abnormalities, it is no longer essential to test the chromosomes of the abortus. As we explained earlier, it is much more important to test the chromosomes of the parents for a possible translocation. In such a case the genetic defect in the fetus will not have been due to chance.

Thus, if you find it unpleasant to save the material, you need not feel that you have lost anything in the search for a reason for your miscarriage problem. But having the tissue may be useful in determining whether any tissue still remains in the uterus. This will help you and your physician decide if you need a D and C.

SUMMARY

1. The abnormality in the fetus that leads to a miscarriage can come from one of the parents' germ cells (ovum or sperm), or as an entirely new *(de novo)* event in the very early life of the embryo. Most genetic defects probably arise from the ovum or sperm.

2. Most of these genetic errors are due to random, "badluck" events.

3. There is some chance that the environment in which you work or live is contributing to your miscarriage problem. You should avoid chemicals, drugs, and radiation during pregnancy.

4. Genetic analysis of both parents involves a blood test, in which the cells are analyzed for genetic errors. If one or both parents carries a translocation (genetic error) that they are passing on to the fetus, this can be discovered with this test.

5. Amniocentesis during pregnancy can tell you if the baby has a genetic defect. It is relatively safe—that is, the risk of spontaneous abortion is only about 2 to 5 percent.

6. Most of the random events that cause genetic abnormalities in the fetus, and thus spontaneous abortions, occur during chromosome division or migration. For this reason it is generally not important to test the chromosomes of the aborted fetus—it is more important to test the chromosomes of the parents.

VI

Other Causes of
Spontaneous Abortion

In Chapter 5 we suggested that about 50 percent of all first-trimester abortions are caused by genetic errors. (Translocations account only for about 5 percent of these; the rest seem to be the result of chance events.) The causes of the other 50 percent of these miscarriages, however, are much less apparent. Various hypotheses have been suggested. These include hormonal dysfunction, uterine abnormalities, infection, exposure to chemicals and radiation, drugs, psychogenic factors, nutritional deficiencies, and traumatic injury.

HORMONAL, ENDOCRINE, AND
IMMUNOLOGICAL DYSFUNCTIONS

The problem of inadequate progesterone production is often called corpus-luteum deficiency because the hormone comes from the part of the ovary called the corpus luteum. It is produced in large amounts after ovulation and functions to thicken and mature the uterine endometrium (inner lining of the uterus) so that it can accommodate the fertilized egg.

The diagnosis of corpus-luteum inadequacy is made by hormone assay of the blood and/or urine, and by a sampling of the post-ovulatory endometrium. The tissue is obtained by biopsy when the woman is not pregnant and sent to the lab for analysis. Physical evidence of poor maturation of the endometrium will confirm the suspicion raised by low progesterone levels in the blood and urine. In addition a graph of basal body temperature can be used to chart ovulation, since it is known that the woman's temperature will rise in response to the production of progesterone.

The usefulness of this procedure in cases of habitual spontaneous abortion is still debated. There is no consensus that corpus-luteum inadequacy is responsible for habitual spontaneous abortions, or even that it exists at all. Moreover, as we said earlier, the FDA does not recommend that progesterone-type drugs be used to treat the problem. In spite of this some physicians do give medroxyprogesterone (Provera®) or injections of progesterone after ovulation in an attempt to promote the maturation of the endometrium. It should be noted that large doses of progesterone have been shown to decrease the normal production of this hormone by the body. Thus the treatment may be counterproductive.

Virtually every obstetrician will order a glucose-tolerance test for a patient who has had repeated miscarriages. This is a test for diabetes, which involves drinking a large dose of sugar (glucose) and taking repeated blood-sugar levels to check the ability of the pancreas to produce insulin and clear the sugar from the bloodstream. It is now apparent that this test is of little or no diagnostic benefit for the woman who has had repeated spontaneous abortions. It has become part of standard medical practice though, and many physicians would feel uncomfortable if they did not order the test—thus possibly leaving themselves open to a charge of malpractice. The results are not often very productive.

Thyroid disease has also been suggested as a contributor to the spontaneous-abortion problem. In the original study, performed in 1951, low thyroid-hormone production was linked to spontaneous abortion in about half the subjects. This claim makes little or no sense in light of our current understanding of the genetic causes we discussed in Chapter 6.

Moreover, patients who are markedly deficient in thyroid hormone will show other symptoms long before the problem of recurrent miscarriage even arises. Ordering thyroid hormone studies has also become part of standard medical practice, but these tests are fairly expensive and have not proved to be of diagnostic value.

Systemic lupus erythematosus is an autoimmune disease in which the immune system is defective and attacks the blood vessels and other tissues. It has been said that the incidence of miscarriage goes up in persons who have clinically apparent lupus. Lupus is rare, compared to the number of spontaneous abortions, and not likely to be important in the investigation of recurrent abortions. By the time symptoms are evident in lupus, there is ample reason to do blood tests for its presence. It is probably not worthwhile to perform such tests on everyone who has had recurrent abortions unless other signs of the disease are present.

Some investigation is going on into the potential immunological causes of habitual spontaneous abortion. For an immunologist the fetus has an unusual relationship to the mother, in that it is a foreign body that is *not* rejected during pregnancy. In that sense it is a graft or transplant that succeeds naturally. Our experience of the surgical transplantation of organs like the kidney, heart, skin, and cornea indicates that this is a very unusual situation. Normally when a foreign substance or organ is introduced into the body, it is the task of the immune system to reject that substance. When transplant surgery is performed, powerful blocking drugs must be used to prevent this rejection.

In the case of pregnancy the transplant occurs successfully without these drugs. It has been demonstrated that the mother's own body produces a blocking substance thought to be necessary for maintaining pregnancy. This substance has been found to be lacking in women who have had recurrent abortions. However, these studies are in an early stage of development, and only a small number of cases have been investigated.

The exact role of this blocking substance and the precise effects of its absence in women who miscarry are not well understood. It is possible that the blocking substance is produced only in response to signals from a normal fetus. Thus a genetically abnormal fetus may not send the mother the proper signal to activate the production of this substance (an IgG—an immunoglobulin like the gamma globulin that is administered if you are exposed to hepatitis). In this instance it would not be a malfunction of the mother's immune system that brings about the miscarriage, but an abnormality in the fetus. Further, it is not known whether the blocking substance is produced only in response to a baby that is carried to term. Thus, a series of pregnancies aborted in the first trimester might not have stimulated the mother's immune system at all.

In short this research is new and exciting, but not yet of therapeutic or diagnostic value. Immunological tests for women with recurrent spontaneous abortions are purely experimental and not part of a regular testing procedure. Most physicians and hospitals do not have access to these tests, so if you are asked to participate in such a testing program, it will almost certainly be for research purposes. Future work in this area may be productive, but as yet it is too early to tell.

There are other kinds of immunological rejections that have been proposed as causes of miscarriage. The best-known involve the ABO and Rh blood groups. The research goes back as far as 1925, when it was noted that fewer babies with blood type A were born to type-A fathers and type-B mothers than was predicted by simple probability. This implied to the researchers that these babies had been aborted.

We become type A, B, AB, or O because of large sugarlike molecules that are located on the outside of our red blood cells. We inherit the typing from our parents. Although it may be demonstrated by statistical analysis that parents with particular blood types have fewer children of a particular type than would be expected, this is not proof that this incompatibility causes spontaneous abortions.

A similar incompatibility can exist between a mother whose blood lacks the Rh factor (Rh-negative) and her baby, whose blood will probably be Rh-positive if the father's is also. This has also been suggested as a possible cause of miscarriage, but Rh disease is in reality more of a problem in the third trimester and in the newborn. Babies with Rh incompatibility suffer from a hemolytic anemia that originates when the mother's sensitized immune system attacks the infant's red blood cells. This is unlikely to be a cause of recurrent first-trimester spontaneous abortions.

In sum, it is probably not helpful for you to undergo testing for the endocrine disorders (thyroid, diabetes), lupus, or immunological deficiencies in the search for the cause of your miscarriage problem. Furthermore, corpus-luteum inadequacy is no longer with certainty seen as a cause of first-trimester abortions. Diagnostic tests, including endometrial biopsy for the purpose of analyzing corpus-luteum function, are therefore probably not indicated—especially since treatment with progesterone is not advised.

ANATOMICAL ABNORMALITIES

A few women have incomplete or imperfect physical development of the uterus and vagina, adhesions inside the uterus (Asherman's syndrome), or myomas (benign tumors of the uterine muscle), all of which have been associated with an increased incidence of miscarriages. While many of these women have been able to carry a normal pregnancy to term, the ease with which these conditions can be uncovered and their amenability to surgical repair have made testing appear to be worthwhile.

It is estimated that about 1 woman in 700 women has some unusual anatomical formation of the uterus or vagina. This abnormality occurs as a result of incomplete development of the Müllerian duct (the structure in the fetal body from which the female reproductive organs originate) during fetal development. Many formations are possible, including a septum (a membranous wall) running down the middle of the uterus, a completely double uterus, a uterus with one horn, or a combination of different entities.

Many, in fact probably most, of these women have normal full-term pregnancies in spite of these abnormalities. They go without detection because no reproductive problem exists. Their role in causing spontaneous abortions is therefore not entirely clear and probably depends on the extent of the anatomical problem. If these problems actually cause miscarriages, it is probably due to a mechanical prevention of normal nidation (nesting), or inadequate accommodation of the growing fetus.

Asherman's syndrome is a condition in which adhesions develop inside the uterus as a result of overly vigorous curettage (scraping) or infection associated with curettage. This somewhat rare condition occurs most often in women who hemorrhage after childbirth and require the D and C to stop the bleeding. After the scraping is performed, the exposed walls of the uterus stick together during the healing process, forming a scarred obstruction to the uterine cavity. It is thought that these adhesions block nesting in a purely mechanical way, by making the uterus smaller and the wall less capable of receiving the fertilized egg.

Even though the overall incidence of these anatomical problems is small and their role in causing spontaneous abortions not entirely clear, they are important because they can be found and corrected with surgery. They are detected by hysterosalpingogram, an X-ray test that involves introducing a contrast dye into the uterus and Fallopian tube.

The test is performed with the patient lying on her back. Generally it is done on a fluoroscopy table, which permits direct visualization of the internal organs at various intervals during the procedure. After a speculum is inserted into the vagina, and the cavity opened, a syringe is introduced into the cervical canal. Dye is then injected into the uterus and Fallopian tubes, and some contrast medium is allowed to spill out into the pelvic area.

Some abnormalities in the pelvic anatomy, or the adhesions of the Asherman syndrome, can be seen on the X ray. These problems can be corrected surgically if it seems likely that they might interfere with normal pregnancy. Many surgeons report good results with these procedures. If you are contemplating surgery, be sure to discuss the pros and cons of the procedure with your surgeon before agreeing to have it done.

It is true that these anatomical problems do not necessarily prevent women from carrying normal pregnancies, but this does not negate the value of these procedures. However, it should help to put them into perspective, since with or without surgical intervention it may be possible to carry your next pregnancy to term. These anatomical problems do not usually cause repeated spontaneous abortions. In the end you and your mate must make this decision in conjunction with your physician. Do not hesitate to get a few other opinions before making your final decision. And if you are uncertain, allow yourself time to wait and rethink the issue. The surgical option never goes away.

It is even more difficult to assess the importance of myomas ("fibroids") in causing spontaneous abortions. Women with very large myomas can carry a pregnancy to term, although some studies do implicate them as a cause of abortions. Myomas are also sometimes detectable on hysterosalpingograms and can be surgically removed.

The myomas that are important here are probably those *inside* the uterus (subserous). You may need X-ray studies or a D and C to substantiate the presence of these myomas inside the uterine cavity.

As with the anatomical problems that we have been discussing, you and your mate will have to evaluate your feelings about surgery to remove a myoma. The decision to undergo corrective surgery should never be rushed. There are many risks involved, and one must balance them against the possible rewards. If you have tried to have children for many years and met with continued frustration, surgery may be an option. But after one or two spontaneous abortions it may be wise to try to become pregnant again before considering an operation. In general the odds will be on your side, although this, of course, depends on the extent of the abnormality and each case must be evaluated individually.

INFECTION

It has been known for many years that infections can cause spontaneous abortions in other animals and birth defects in humans. Some infectious agents have been implicated in causing *fetal wastage*, i.e. pregnancy loss. *Brucella abortus* is a bacterium specifically named for its ability to cause miscarriages in cattle, goats, and swine. *Listeria monocytogenes* and *Toxoplasmosis gondii* are other organisms that have been associated with miscarriages. While much has been written about these agents and their role in causing spontaneous abortions it is controversial whether they play a role in causing the problem for humans.

Viruses have also been thought to cause miscarriages. Studies have been conducted in which women were asked if they had had a viral infection (like a cold or flu) prior to their spontaneous abortion, and attempts have been made to correlate these findings with the miscarriage rate. These studies depend on the selective memory of the patient and probably have no value in assessing the problem.

Rubella (German measles), cytomegalovirus, and herpes simplex virus are known to be capable of causing damage to a developing fetus and hence could be potential causes of spontaneous abortion. Again the role of these viral agents is not clear at all. There has been a widespread effort to educate the public about the danger of exposure to rubella during the first 12 weeks of pregnancy. It is at this time that the infection can cause severe birth defects. However, most of the thrust has been to prevent the birth of abnormal children, and not to prevent miscarriages. It is unlikely that rubella plays an important role in causing repeated spontaneous abortions.

If you are thinking about becoming pregnant, it is possible to have a blood test to see if you have an immunity to rubella. If you have had rubella in the past, either with or without symptoms, you have antibodies in your blood that will prevent you from contracting the infection. If you do not have this immunological protection, you can receive a vaccination that will stimulate the production of these antibodies in your own body. But if you do not want to receive immunization, you must be quite certain to avoid exposure to rubella, since the chances of having a severely deformed baby are quite high if you are infected early in pregnancy. Even though the rubella virus is not likely to be the cause of repeated sponta-

neous abortions, adequate protection against the infection
should be a concern for all women of childbearing age.

Mycoplasmas, of which there are a number of infectious
strains, have also been suggested as potential causes of repeated spontaneous abortions. Mycoplasmas are microscopic
organisms that have qualities similar to those of both viruses
and bacteria. They often live in the body without causing
noticeable problems. However, a number of strains have been
associated with pregnancy loss. The T-strain mycoplasma has
received substantial attention in this regard, from the point of
view both of miscarriages and of infertility. However, again,
there is no definitive proof.

Mycoplasmas are normally found in the vagina and cervix
of more than 50 percent of pregnant women in this country.
Since most of these women have no abortion problem, finding the organism in the reproductive tract is not proof that it
causes spontaneous abortion. Commonly it is sought in the
tissue sample that is taken from the uterus for hormone assay.
Even in the uterus it is fairly common, so it would be difficult
to say with certainty that it is causing your miscarriage problem.

Because mycoplasma infections can be treated easily with
antibiotics (tetracyclines most often), many obstetricians choose
this route when confronted with a woman who has a habitual
abortion problem. Again this points to the difficulties that
exist in treating couples who want very much to have children
but continue to abort. Since the data conflicts, most couples
seem to want the treatment. It does offer some hope in an
area where few therapeutic options exist.

In general the risk in taking tetracycline is small. It does
cross the placenta and may cause retardation of the growth of
the skeleton of the developing fetus. But it is given prior to
pregnancy to eradicate the mycoplasma, so this should not be
cause for concern. For the woman who takes tetracycline
there are various possible side-effects including nausea, vomiting, diarrhea, and vaginal yeast infections. This occurs be-

cause the tetracycline kills bacterial organisms in the vagina that normally suppress the overgrowth of yeasts. When these bacteria are killed, the normal balance is disturbed and the yeasts can multiply without having to compete with the other flora (microorganisms) that are usually present.

Syphilis, once thought to be a cause of recurrent spontaneous abortions, is no longer considered significant. As with diabetes and thyroid disease, it is common for all women who abort to have a blood test for syphilis. But the facts indicate that this is not an important cause of the problem, hence the test may not be diagnostically relevant.

In assessing the overall role of infections in causing spontaneous abortions, we are posed with a difficult problem. We have evidence that many agents can cause miscarriages in other animals, yet we have no such direct evidence in humans. Furthermore, we do have some evidence linking various organisms with damage to the fetus, and we know that abnormalities in the fetus can trigger spontaneous abortions. Since treating the mycoplasma infection is relatively easy and inexpensive, most couples and physicians do so to try to rule out that potential risk. However, there is no hard evidence to prove that treating these infections is worthwhile.

ACCIDENTS AND INJURIES

Except for the rare severe injury, there is no reason to think that spontaneous abortions are caused by accidental trauma to the abdomen. Many women claim that a blow to the abdomen, a fall, vigorous intercourse, or horseback riding caused their miscarriage, but there is no scientific evidence to support this.

There have been reports in the medical literature of spontaneous abortion following abdominal surgery (laparotomy) or automobile accidents. These involved genetically normal fetuses and hence might have been precipitated by the traumatic event.

Less serious accidents or injuries—although they do not in any sense cause miscarriages—may still have important psychological and emotional implications. For example, a woman who blames her miscarriage on a fall suffered during pregnancy may, consciously or unconsciously, be concealing deeper feelings about the miscarriage itself that she is unable to contend with. Such explanations of the cause of a miscarriage may signal that other issues are at stake. These deeper feelings need to be explored on an emotional level. But there is no reason to expect that minor injury—either physical or emotional—causes miscarriages.

DRUGS, CHEMICALS, AND X-RAY EXPOSURE

We discussed this in Chapter 5. The most important point to remember is that many drugs, chemicals such as petroleum products (insecticides, plastics, organic solvents, etc.), and X rays are all capable of damaging chromosomes. There is no hard evidence linking these agents to the actual spontaneous abortion rate, and radiologists in general do not advise abortion after diagnostic X rays during pregnancy. Yet caution during pregnancy is always advised. When the fetus is in its embryonic form the chromosomes are multiplying rapidly and hence are especially vulnerable to insult by toxic agents.

NUTRITION

Some researchers have hypothesized that vitamin and protein deficiencies can cause spontaneous abortions. If this is true, the problem is a rare one in the United States. Some pregnant women may have poor dietary intake of essential nutrients, but extreme malnutrition is unusual.

It has been suggested that the incidence of spontaneous abortion rises during famines and wartime when food is extremely scarce. It is obviously very difficult to study these kinds of situations because the entire society is disorganized. An important point to emphasize is that the developing fetus will take essential nutrients from the mother's supply of stored vitamins, minerals and protein to maintain intrauterine growth. The pregnant woman's body is therefore under added stress during periods of food deprivation. Thus, while we cannot say with certainty that nutritional deficiencies can cause spontaneous abortions, it seems wise to consider this as a factor. We cannot say at this time whether the abortion results from a retardation of fetal growth or the inability of the weakened mother to carry the pregnancy.

In any case a good diet during pregnancy is very important, both for the mother and the fetus. We will discuss this more in Chapter 11.

THE ROLE OF MEDICAL TESTS AND THERAPY

Far less is known concretely about the causes of spontaneous abortions than we would like. This lack of medical and scientific information—even in light of the statistical reality that most couples will eventually have normal pregnancies—is frustrating for the patient and the physician. The fact is that although many different substances and diseases have been suspected to cause miscarriage, the relationship has not been proved in most of these cases.

The two entities considered most important in the medical investigation are the genetic and the anatomical causes. Therefore it seems logical to do chromosomal analysis of the parents and possibly a hysterosalpingogram of the woman. Even though it is not possible to correct a chromosomal abnormality (balanced translocation), it is important for parents to know of its presence. This information, combined with good genetic counseling (and possibly amniocentesis), gives the prospective parents a better chance of evaluating their problem fully. Anatomical abnormalities are important to uncover, because they can be surgically corrected.

When you begin to receive medical attention for your miscarriage problem, you will have to make many decisions about which tests and therapies you want to undergo. Discuss all the issues between yourselves and with your physician. Get other medical opinions if you feel uncomfortable, and use the data we have presented to ask informed questions about the reasons for each test and therapeutic regimen. Remember that sometimes physicians order tests out of habit, or for medical-legal reasons you may not agree with. Try to be discerning consumers and take an active role in your medical care.

INCOMPETENT CERVIX

Recurrent spontaneous abortions that occur in the second-trimester of pregnancy (fourteenth to twenty-eighth week) tend to involve genetically normal fetuses. These late miscarriages therefore have different causes and different treatments from the first-trimester miscarriages we have been discussing so far. Though late miscarriages are much less common, they are important because of their amenability to surgical treatment.

These second-trimester abortions usually involve a rapid, relatively bloodless, and painless event. The woman often does not experience the cramping, contractions, or dilation and effacement of the cervix that are characteristic of the early miscarriages, because the element of labor is not present. Moreover, these events come rapidly, whereas many first-trimester spontaneous abortions occur over days of interrupted bleeding and contractions.

These abortions are often considered to be caused by an *incompetent cervix*. This means that the cervix is not able to hold up under the increasing weight of the fetus and amniotic fluid that accumulate during the second trimester of pregnancy. An incompetent cervix is a second-trimester problem because it is at this time that the fetus and fluid increase dramatically in weight. During the first 14 weeks most of the growth involves the uterus in response to the increasing amounts of estrogen and progesterone that are produced.

Making the diagnosis of an incompetent cervix is not always easy. The picture is quite clear when the pregnant woman, in her second trimester, is found to have the bag of waters (amniotic sac) bulging from the cervix. In such a case it is fairly obvious that the cervix can no longer remain closed under the weight of the uterine contents.

An incompetent cervix can also be diagnosed prior to a next pregnancy. If the woman has a history of one or more second-trimester abortions, the suspicion of an incompetent cervix is raised. Next the physician can do a physical examination, and if a probe (number 8 Hegar dilator or similar-sized catheter) can be passed through the internal cervical os with relative ease, there is further indication of an incompetent cervix. Finally the physician can order a hysterosalpingogram to confirm the apparent dilation of the os.

There are a number of causes of cervical incompetence. Sometimes the problem is simply congenital. In other words, some women are born with a weak cervical ring that cannot maintain itself during pregnancy. Sometimes women develop the problem after an extremely difficult vaginal birth, where the cervix suffers laceration by an extremely large and rapidly expelled infant. In some cases the problem is caused by excessive medical manipulation of the cervix during a D and

C, or after biopsy of (cutting a tissue sample from) the cervix. These two problems can sometimes be avoided when more care is taken during these procedures. However, if the extent of the cervical abnormality is such that an extensive biopsy is necessary, it may not be possible to avoid incompetent cervix.

Even without physical or X-ray evidence of cervical dilation, many physicians will want to do a surgical repair of the cervix of a patient with a history of second-trimester miscarriages. That is because it is a therapeutic option in an area where few alternatives exist. The procedures for repair have varying degrees of success, depending on the patients selected for study and the surgeon performing the procedure. Success rates vary between 40 and 90 percent. However, these studies are hard to evaluate because many women will carry a subsequent pregnancy without surgery.

The repair involves surgically reinforcing the cervix with sutures (stitches). There are four common variations on the procedure (Wurm, Lash, Shirodkar, MacDonald), each of which reinforces the lower part of the uterus. The sutures must be placed high up in the cervix and stitched tightly enough to give support to the cervix without cutting off blood circulation to the tissues.

The timing of the procedure is important. Generally it is performed in the second trimester, after the danger of first-trimester abortion has passed. However, some physicians do them between pregnancies. But they should be done before the membranes bulge or bleeding commences. Furthermore, they should not be attempted after 32 weeks of pregnancy.

At 38 weeks of pregnancy, or at the onset of labor, the sutures must be cut. Failure to do so may result in rupture of the uterus, as labor contractions are strong. Some people elect to have Caesarean sections rather than having the sutures cut. You should come to an understanding about this with your physician if you want to have a vaginal delivery and have undergone one of these suturing procedures.

In circumstances where the procedure is not performed before the thirty-second week of pregnancy, it is advisable for the woman to try bed rest and avoid surgery. Sometimes the resting position that is employed is the Trendelenburg, in which the hips are raised slightly above the head. This is designed to relieve the cervix of the weight of the fetus and fluid. Since it is not a comfortable position for long periods, one should expect to shift into other positions at times.

Though few women are affected by the problem of cervical incompetence, we have discussed it here because it is amenable to treatment. Its origins in excessive medical manipulation of the cervix during various procedures should alert the practitioner to the importance of using care when doing a D and C or cone biopsy of the cervix.

SUMMARY

1. Many diseases—e.g., thyroid disease, diabetes, syphilis—have been thought to cause recurrent spontaneous abortions. The present view is that these diseases are rarely significant in causing miscarriages. Medical tests for these conditions are therefore probably not helpful.

2. Immunological rejection based on ABO, Rh, or other blood incompatibilities are most probably not major contributors to the miscarriage problem. New research into an immunological blocking factor may one day prove helpful, but it is now only in the research stage.

3. There are various anatomical abnormalities that can cause spontaneous abortions for purely mechanical reasons. These problems can be uncovered with X-ray

testing (hysterosalpingogram) and are often amenable to surgical correction.

4. No one knows with certainty whether bacterial, mycoplasma, or viral infections cause miscarriages in humans, although they are known to do so in domestic animals. Treatment for mycoplasma infections is often employed because the treatment is easy, inexpensive, and relatively safe.

5. Traumatic injury, other than severe injury from automobile accidents or surgery, is not likely to be a cause of spontaneous abortion. Similarly, nutritional deficiencies, short of starvation, are not likely to cause recurrent abortions.

6. Relatively quick, bloodless, and painless second-trimester abortions are considered to be caused by an incompetent cervix. Various surgical procedures are available to strengthen the cervix and may increase your ability to carry a future pregnancy.

VII

An Abortion
Threatens

As you probably know from personal experience, a miscarriage begins with vaginal bleeding. When you start to bleed and your cervix is closed this is called a *threatened abortion*. This is the term that your doctor is likely to use. While estimates vary, somewhere between 25 and 50 percent of women bleed, or more accurately *spot*, sometime during pregnancy. Though only half of these women will go on to miscarry, any bleeding should be considered a threatened abortion. It is a sign that you should not take lightly, even though your chances of having a normal child are still very good.

A THREATENED ABORTION
(MISCARRIAGE) BEGINS

During pregnancy, spotting must start from somewhere. In fact it can come from the vagina, or the surrounding structures of cervix, uterus, or urethra. While bleeding of any kind during pregnancy should be considered a serious warning sign, not every case will be an impending spontaneous abortion.

If the bleeding is coming from the vagina due to some local problem, this is not going to be a miscarriage. Most of the time this bleeding is slight, but spotting during pregnancy is also sometimes very slight. You simply cannot tell where the bleeding is coming from unless someone does a pelvic exam and looks inside the vagina.

The blood could also be coming from your cervix, due to an erosion, polyp, or cancer. Again the bleeding is generally slight, but there is no way of telling that it is an erosion until someone looks at the cervix. There could even be some blood on your underpants if you have a urinary-tract infection and dribble a small amount of urine. If you do have a bladder infection, you probably will feel some pain when you urinate and you are likely to be urinating more frequently. But occasionally these symptoms are not totally reliable, and you may have a urinary infection with few obvious signs. Early in pregnancy you often urinate more frequently, and this is normal, so this again may be confusing.

All this should make sense if you look back at the anatomical diagram in Chapter 4, Figure 1, and realize that any of the organs in and around the vagina can bleed. Bleeding can also come from the rectum, due to hemorrhoids, which are common during pregnancy. You just cannot know the cause of the bleeding until someone examines you.

Spotting between the fourth and sixth weeks of pregnancy can signal an ectopic pregnancy. The cells in this case actually implant themselves in the Fallopian tube or some other surrounding structure outside the uterus. An ectopic pregnancy is generally painful, in fact very painful, because the tube is sensitive after being stretched by the growing ball of cells. If you have an ectopic pregnancy that ruptures the tube, it will not only be quite painful but will also require surgery. This is a dangerous situation and another reason why you should be examined by an experienced medical person if you bleed while you are pregnant.

Once it has been established that you do not have any of these problems, then statistically you are most likely to be having a *threatened abortion*.

Only time will tell exactly what is going to happen. If you do not go on to miscarry, then one can only conjecture about the reasons why you had some vaginal bleeding. The physiological reasons for this are not completely clear. Most probably the bleeding comes from the placental area. There is a theory that dropping progesterone levels may also cause bleeding. A common cause of bleeding may also be the nidation process, when the fertilized egg burrows into the uterine lining.

If you do not miscarry, you probably will never know, since it is not possible to look directly inside the uterus without possibly disturbing the pregnancy. A hands-off policy is generally advised. The best thing to do is wait, relax, rest, and see what happens.

IS IT AN INEVITABLE ABORTION?

This is a point that is debated by the medical profession. Is there such a thing as an inevitable abortion? In other words when you are examined by your doctor, can he or she tell whether or not you will actually go on to miscarry?

Many physicians say that there is no such thing as an inevitable abortion. They take the humble approach and admit that there are always exceptions in medicine. It is easy to be fooled by one's predictions, so the more cautious doctors try not to predict. With potential miscarriages this is probably the wisest approach to take.

Dr. Rothchild stated this well:

A *threatened miscarriage* (abortion) means that there are symptoms that are associated with losing the pregnancy, but I can't say at this time which way it is going to go. *Inevitable* means that they are having some symptoms and physical findings which mean to me that they are definitely going to miscarry.

I say this with a certain amount of humility, because I had the personal experience of a woman who had what I thought was an inevitable abortion who absolutely refused a D and C.

She wanted the baby tremendously and we held off and she carried the baby to term. I learned a tremendous amount from that, because according to our criteria we should have done a D and C.

In my experience, nevertheless, if tissue has been passed, or if the cervix is greatly dilated and thinned out, a miscarriage is probably inevitable.

What we are saying is that little if anything in medicine is necessarily inevitable. Although you may have many ominous signs indicating that your pregnancy is not proceeding normally, it is usually best not to try to predict what is going to happen. While all of this waiting may be emotionally and physically painful, you should try to remember that in the end you will not be physically harmed by these events and you may see your pregnancy continue to term.

SIGNS OF AN ABNORMAL PREGNANCY

What kind of things will your physician be concerned with when she or he examines you?

The first thing is whether or not the uterus is enlarging normally. For each week of pregnancy there should be appropriate enlargement of your uterus. If your uterus feels small on physical-examination, it is an important indication that the fetus is not growing normally. Such a growth disorder may be due to a genetic problem or difficulty during nidation such as we discussed in Chapter 5, and it may be an early sign of a miscarriage.

The bimanual portion of the pelvic examination is useful in assessing the maturation of the fetus. It includes feeling the abdomen and feeling the cervix and uterus through the vagina. The size of the uterus is important for dating the pregnancy. Whether or not the cervix is dilated can also be determined in this way. Women often cannot remember the exact date of their last menstrual period or cannot give a reasonable guess as to when conception occurred. For these reasons it is necessary to do the exam. When the same examiner does a number of exams over a few weeks, it becomes more reliable as a way of dating pregnancy.

Further information comes from the speculum exam. This is the way your cervix and vagina are directly viewed by the examiner. It involves inserting a speculum into the vagina and opening the vaginal cavity. A speculum is a metal or plastic instrument with two arms that swing on a fulcrum. When inserted into the vagina it can be opened, thereby spreading the walls of the vagina and bringing the cervix and vaginal cavity into view.

Remember that we said an early miscarriage is like labor. It is a no-choice event in which the fetus is expelled from the uterus by strong muscular contractions. To do this, the mouth of the uterus (cervix) must be open to allow the fetus to pass.

This process of opening is called dilation and effacement. *Effacement* means that the tissues of the cervix must thin out and stretch to form an opening. *Dilation* means simply "opening," or "widening." So when the medical person performs the bimanual exam and feels your cervix, he or she will be trying to gauge the amount of dilation and effacement of the cervix.

Both dilation and effacement are necessary for the fetus to pass out of the uterus, and both processes usually happen at the same time. Imagine trying to push a ball out of a rubber balloon whose opening is tightly shut. To force the ball out, the balloon's mouth and neck must stretch (efface) as well as open. When your cervix does this, it is going through much the same process that it does when you birth a baby. For some women both the contractions and the process of opening can be painful. Like labor, the amount of pain is individual. Some women find it hardly painful at all, while other women find it very painful. If you do feel pain, there is medication available to help relieve you of some of the discomfort.

It may or may not be difficult for the examiner to judge how likely you are to miscarry, even after the pelvic exam. If your cervix is markedly open, if there is ample effacement, and if tissue has passed, then one can say with a fair degree of certainty that a miscarriage will occur. However, like most things in medicine, it is the gray areas that predominate, and it may not be obvious which way events will actually turn out. Again, only time and waiting will tell.

An important point here is that the amount of bleeding that you have is not a good indication of the likelihood of your miscarrying. One obstetrician told us of a woman who actually required transfusions because she bled profusely, yet went on to deliver a normal baby months later. Some women on the other hand spot slightly and then pass the fetus. There are as many variations in the amount of bleeding during a threatened miscarriage as there are women who bleed.

TESTS TO PREDICT A MISCARRIAGE

There are two medical tests that may help considerably in predicting the outcome of your threatened abortion. One set of tests has to do with the hormones that are necessary to maintain pregnancy—HCG and progesterone. The second, ultrasound, which gives a picture of the inside of the uterus, can tell you about the position and development of the placenta and the fetus. These tests are not always available. This depends on the facilities of your community, hospital, or doctor's office.

In Chapter 4 we discussed the role of both progesterone and HCG (human chorionic gonadotropin) in maintaining pregnancy. Both hormones are present in the mother's body in measurable amounts which increase during pregnancy. If they do not increase, or in fact fall, this is a fairly reliable indication that you will abort.

Different women produce different amounts of progesterone and HCG. A moderate level for one woman may represent a low level for another woman. To make the best use of the tests, it is important to take readings of these hormones prior to the onset of vaginal bleeding.

By taking readings over the early course of the pregnancy, you can compare the numerical values and see if the amounts are increasing. If you begin to bleed, the levels that are obtained can be compared to the previous week's results. A drop in the amounts of these hormones is an ominous sign. It is the comparison of the numbers that is important, not the exact number itself.

Ultrasound is a diagnostic technique that is being used more and more in obstetrics. It involves passing high-frequency, short-wavelength sound waves through the uterus and its contents. The transmission pattern of these sound waves can be electronically resolved into a picture of the position and development of the fetus and placenta.

The ultrasonic waves bounce off the various structures (uterus, placenta, amniotic fluid, fetus) in different ways depending on the density of the materials. Echoes of the sound waves are then analyzed as they are reflected back onto a receiver. The pattern of the echoes can be projected onto a screen or photographed. This can give you important information about the size and position of the fetus and the contents of the pregnancy sac, and can tell you if you are going to have twins. The absence of a sac, an empty sac, or a large clot are signs that a miscarriage is likely.

The most commonly used ultrasound device today is the B-scanner. With this type of machine the sound beam is moved along the skin and a two-dimensional picture is made. When this picture is taken at different depths, a three-dimensional view results. The embryonic sac can be seen as early as the fifth or sixth week of pregnancy and the embryo itself a bit later.

There are both pros and cons to using ultrasound. No one knows the possible dangers of passing high-energy sound waves through a small, developing fetus. It is known that sound energy passing through tissue (at a higher energy level than normally used in obstetrics) causes it to heat up and bubble, forming small cavities. Further it is known that sound energy can disrupt the molecular structure of DNA, the chemical basis of the genetic code. To date most doctors think that ultrasound is very safe and use it commonly in obstetrics. However, there is always some element of doubt when you do anything to the human body—especially during the very early and sensitive stages of embryonic life.

Furthermore, ultrasound may not always give you an answer that is completely reliable. The sac may be poorly visualized or completely obscured. In this case the information may not help assess the viability of your pregnancy. It is estimated that ultrasound is 80 percent accurate for analyzing first-trimester pregnancies. But where spontaneous abortion is concerned, 20 percent is a large margin of error.

In many hospitals ultrasound is used frequently during pregnancy, while in others it is either unavailable or more cautiously employed. This is a relatively new procedure, and with time we will gain greater knowledge of its usefulness and safety. For now it is a decision that you should make with your physician.

To sum up the role of ultrasound, let us portray two opposite obstetric views. Both these physicians are interested in high-risk problems, like spontaneous abortions, and both are active in major teaching hospitals. In short, both are extremely knowledgeable, competent, sensitive medical practitioners, yet they have different ideas of what is best. Read their thoughts and decide for yourself what you think is best for your pregnancy.

Dr. A, who is in favor of using ultrasound when an abortion threatens, said:

> [When a patient is spotting] bed rest is the only simple-minded thing that works. If the spotting stops, get an ultrasound and see what you are dealing with. Find out whether there is a pregnancy there or not. Fifty percent of the people are not affected by bed rest, and that is why I want to go promptly to ultrasound and see what you are dealing with. . . .
>
> If you have spotting and you get an ultrasound, and you find out that there is no longer a sac and essentially you already have dead products of conception, then there is no sense in sitting around in bed. You can show that there is a drop in chorionic gonadotropins to convince the woman that she lost the pregnancy, and you can do a D and C so that you can study the material so you can see why.
>
> But if your spotting is coming because your placenta is advancing and there simply is bleeding at that point, you might not want to be maximally physically active. You might want to take it easy for a while. I would agree that it is a pretty old-fashioned treatment, but if you combine it with ultrasound it can make some sense.

Dr. B is against using ultrasound to diagnose a threatened abortion, for these reasons:

> Ultrasound has a reasonable false-positive and false-negative result. Ultrasound is not 100 percent certain. I would be very upset if I did a D and C and found a good pregnancy. I have done [elective] abortions, so that is not my objection. What upsets me is that I might have terminated a pregnancy that the woman really wanted and could possibly have carried to term.
>
> If I don't see the sac on ultrasound, it doesn't mean that it is not there. I don't know what ultrasound does, so I try to avoid it. I am pretty convinced that it is a safe modality [procedure], but there still may be a very small risk. If the risk is very small, is the risk worth being able to tell the woman whether there is an intact sac? I don't know that it is.
>
> I don't make these decisions anymore. At least not alone. I ask the people to join in on them, and we make it together. Even with an intact sac, she may miscarry. There may be quite a nice sac with blood in the uterus obscuring it. There may be echoes obscuring the sac, and I certainly wouldn't interrupt the pregnancy anyway.
>
> Sometimes people ask me, "Should I get it over with [do a D and C]?" They may have been bleeding for the fourth day already, and it may be the second time in the pregnancy that they are bleeding.
>
> They ask me, "What if I let this pregnancy go on, will I have difficulty and will the baby be normal?" The answer is that the outcome is no more likely to be abnormal than that of the general population. One study I know of concluded that there were fewer abnormalities [in spontaneous aborters] than in the general population. I presume that those that really had a problem miscarried and selected out the abnormal babies. So if

that is what you are worried about, that is not a reason to interrupt the pregnancy. You are no different from someone who didn't bleed.

That is important to them. They will hold on a little longer, and in fact the bleeding may stop. I don't like the term *inevitable abortion,* because I'm not sure I can make the diagnosis with a reasonable degree of certainty.

You now have read two fairly conflicting views. If either ultrasound or hormone testing is available to you, you must make up your own mind. Neither test can tell you with complete certainty what will happen with your threatened abortion. You must evaluate the risks and rewards and make up your own mind. It is best to do this after you have carefully considered the feelings of those who are close to you and the advice of your physician.

Once your pregnancy test (a urinary HCG test) has turned negative, it is assumed that the fetus is dead and that you will abort. In this instance your physician may suggest doing a D and C to terminate the pregnancy. We will talk more about the D and C later. For now it is enough to say that the current medical view is that an abortion is inevitable only after a negative pregnancy test and the passage of tissue.

BED REST

Bed rest and avoiding sexual intercourse are the only ways of averting a threatened abortion if there has already been some bleeding. Whether or not they do any good is debated, but at least they do no harm. In medicine that is important. There is an axiom that everyone learns during his or her medical training—*do no harm*.

Does bed rest mean that you cannot get out of bed to go to the bathroom? Does it mean that you should take your meals in bed? Does it mean that you should feel and act like a complete invalid?

No, it merely means that you are to rest and wait to see what happens. If you are bleeding because the placenta is growing inside the uterus, bed rest is intended to give the placenta the best chance of reattaching itself securely to the uterine lining. If you move around, you might make this implantation process a bit more difficult.

Since we do not know with absolute certainty why most women miscarry, there is little reason to think that bed rest will help the placenta with implantation. All of this is conjecture in the face of an unclear scientific understanding. No one can tell you that a trip to the bathroom, eating at the dinner table, or any other activity is going to cause you to abort. It may appear to you that you pass more clots and blood after you stand up. This is probably the effect of gravity causing the blood to flow downward and not of additional damage that you are doing. The role of bed rest is based on our *lack* of knowledge, an inability to provide a medical cure, and the assured knowledge that rest will not harm you or your pregnancy.

Dr. Rothchild put bed rest into this context:

> I tell patients to have bed rest for tradition's sake only. The way that I do it is this. Because women blame themselves I say, obstetricians recommend bed rest and not having intercourse or putting anything in the vagina in cases of threatened abortion. But we have no evidence that it has any effect. It is the only thing that we know to tell people.
>
> That gives her permission to rest in bed, but not to feel guilty about it if she can't. A lot of women who you say go stay in bed to have a one-year-old, a two-year-old and a three-year-old, and a husband who works nine to five. She can't stay in bed. And I can't say that it really has an effect.

If you cannot rest because of the needs of your family or because it makes you more upset to stay in bed, do not feel guilty. No one can honestly say that the outcome of your pregnancy will be very much changed because you rested or did not rest. In times of stress all of us must find our own way of adjusting. Some women will find resting a comfortable way of dealing with a threatened abortion, while others will find it torture.

For most women a certain amount of bed rest is a natural response to the stress of a threatened miscarriage. In this way it is like any illness—you naturally just do not feel your normal self. So most people reduce their level of activity and wait until they feel well again.

But if this is very stressful for you—if you are the kind of person who needs to be on the go—then it is not really wrong to continue with your usual activity-level. You may have some guilt feelings if you do go on to miscarry, since your physician is likely to have advised rest. You will have to deal with those feelings and possibly the anger of your mate and others, who will see your inability to rest as having increased the likelihood of aborting. You will have to continue to relate to the feelings of your close loved ones long after the experience is over. So you must take their feelings into consideration when you finally make up your mind about how active you should remain during this time.

D AND C

A *D and C* means a *dilation* and *curettage*. Put simply, it involves inserting an instrument into the uterus (through the opening of the cervix) and scraping the inner lining. It is performed under anesthesia. The D and C will be the last part of the miscarriage process. It is done to make certain that all the products of conception (fetus and placenta) are removed from the uterus. This prevents possible bleeding, infection, or infertility, since retained fragments could cause these problems. Though many women will actually pass all of the tissue, it is done to make certain that the spontaneous abortion is complete. It may also be performed to obtain specimens for the pathologist to study.

A D and C ends your pregnancy, so it is important to be sure that the pregnancy has no chance of continuing. Some doctors will not do it unless there is a negative pregnancy test or a serious possibility of danger to the woman. In the situation where bleeding is especially profuse, the D and C prevents a possible hemorrhage. In situations where the abortion appears to be complete, the D and C is a precautionary measure.

You may want the D and C to be done earlier, for instance when you feel that you are bleeding a lot and the miscarriage *feels* inevitable. It is understandable to want to have the entire experience over with as rapidly as possible. But many factors should be considered when you decide to terminate the pregnancy, including the physical exam, a negative pregnancy test, ultrasound, and the symptoms of bleeding and pain. However, remember that once you have the D and C there is always a chance of having terminated a pregnancy that might have succeeded.

Although it is common for women to have D and C's after a spontaneous abortion, there have been few studies to investigate whether the procedure is actually necessary in so many cases. A few physicians wait to see if the woman passes all the products of conception. If it appears that she has, they may put off doing the D and C. A few physicians may wait expectantly to see if hemorrhage or infection results, even if they cannot study the aborted specimen.

Once again this is a decision you must make with your doctor. Many obstetric procedures that were once completely routine are no longer thought to be always necessary. Every procedure, especially those involving general anesthesia, has some element of risk that must be balanced with the potential rewards. Delayed hemorrhage, although rare, is a possibility, but so are operative complications. There is also the element of discomfort and cost in a D and C. In the end you and your close ones, in conjunction with your physician, should decide. Every case is different so there is no single rule that need apply to all unless there is significant risk to the mother's health.

SUMMARY

1. Any bleeding during pregnancy should be considered a threatened abortion.
2. Any bleeding during pregnancy should be brought to the attention of your physician, even if it is a small amount of spotting.
3. No one can predict with certainty whether your threatened abortion will actually go on to be a miscarriage. A good examination of your uterus can give you an idea of whether your pregnancy is progressing normally.
4. Hormone tests for HCG and progesterone can help determine whether your pregnancy is proceeding normally. They are most valuable when you have a series of readings over time.
5. Ultrasound can give you an electronic picture of the pregnancy. It is helpful, but not completely reliable as a prediction of the events to come. We do not know with complete certainty that it is harmless to the developing fetus.

6. A negative pregnancy test is one indication that the pregnancy has ended. At that point you can have a D and C to terminate the spontaneous abortion process surgically with a good assurance that you are not also terminating a potentially normal pregnancy.

VIII

The Woman's Emotions

Probably the most difficult aspect of the miscarriage experience, for me and for the women I've talked with, is the emotional aftermath. This is not to minimize the physical pain. We do suffer physically, sometimes extreme pain, but that is short-term. It ends. The emotional effects go on for a long time afterwards. We go through a range of emotions, some immediate, some long after the physical experience has ended. It may be comforting to know that many of us experience similar responses, although our surroundings and the kinds of help we receive may differ greatly. It's important to remember how unprepared we are (at least initially) to cope with these emotions and how appropriate it is for us to seek help, a great deal of help, to get us through this time. This help can come from our mates, family, friends, doctors and hospital personnel, and others. We will talk about these people in Chapters 9 and 10.

I've talked in earlier chapters about my own immediate

reactions to the three miscarriages I had. My *fear* took two forms. First, I agonized over the chances for the pregnancy to succeed. I didn't give up easily. Each time I bled, I held on to the hope that it would stop and the pregnancy would be saved. I feared losing the pregnancy. The first time only involved a few hours of anxiety, but the second and third miscarriages each followed a week of bleeding and waiting. Those weeks were the longest and most agonizing I have ever known. Rarely have I felt so out of control, so vulnerable.

When I realized that miscarriage was inevitable, my fears turned toward the physical events. I feared what was happening. It hurt! It was very different from anything I'd experienced before. I was bleeding a great deal, which increased my anxiety. Was the pain going to get worse? Was the doctor going to tell me that something even more terrible than the miscarriage was going on in my body? The fear also encompassed the whole hospitalization process. Like many people, I am uncomfortable and nervous in hospitals. The instruments, the alien vocabulary, the intimidating face masks, and sterile environment were all frightening.

Anger was there, too. Why me? I'd done all the right things, especially after the first miscarriage. I'd tried really hard. This was a sudden injustice that I was not ready to handle. Other women succeeded effortlessly; what was happening to me seemed completely unfair. This anger was particularly destructive, since I could only direct it at myself, or as I came to see it, at my body, as separate from my self.

Extreme and profound *disappointment* overwhelmed me each time. The floor was pulled out from under me. My excitement and my hopes were crushed. This was a particularly unremitting disappointment, too. I had learned earlier how to adjust my needs or expectations to fit new situations— part of the process of maturing. Each successive miscarriage, however, made me less able to handle the disappointment. With each miscarriage my emotions became more complex and more difficult to understand. I tried to invest less in the pregnancies as the odds worsened for me, but my desire for another child easily overpowered my self-protective instincts. This kind of forced neutrality—or even worse, ambivalence—adds to the normal uncertainty many women feel about taking on the mother role. With so many emotions at work, it is an extraordinary person who doesn't need help in sorting through them.

Some of the highly charged emotional responses that related to the physical events subsided when the medical crisis passed. The physical fears—of pain, of hemorrhage—ended abruptly with the D and C. A few minutes under general anesthesia and I would wake up *un*pregnant—body in repose, but mind in intense turmoil. Most psychological theorists would agree that the life changes which are most difficult to adjust to are those which happen suddenly, catching us unaware and unprepared. The psyche is strained to its coping limits, in much the same way that the body is strained by sudden change, often adapting by a shock reaction. It's not unusual for women to experience a response lag after the D and C.

For me the disappointment and anger remained after I left the hospital—later they were joined by a host of other unpleasant emotions. There was no transition period. A few hours earlier I had been carrying a baby, doing what I wanted to do and winning everyone's approval. Now, suddenly, I was reduced, cut down. I had become a source of disappointment to myself, to Mark, my family and friends, and others. For probably the first time in my life I felt like a loser. Before I had been fortunate enough to get what I went after. Maybe I had adjusted my goals to fit my potential for success; I had not met with failure in anything that mattered. This surely was failure. A very personal, direct kind of failure. There was no one else to tie it to—the pregnancy was mine, in *my* body, and it didn't work!

By the time of the second miscarriage my self-image was fully involved. This new consciousness of failure in combination with other people's reactions, was rapidly changing how I felt about myself. I began thinking of myself as unfortunate, powerless—or at least, less powerful. The strongest response I found myself eliciting from others was one of *pity*. That was devastating to one who was accustomed to responses at the other end of the spectrum.

I disliked the pity reaction, but wasn't able to redirect it in other people, so I started responding to it. My earlier confidence was eroding, especially in my own body. I found myself in a strange mind-body conflict; I distrusted my body, its signals, its abilities. Since a large part of my concept of myself was naturally tied to my body, that was debilitating to my whole person.

Guilt became a major theme for me. Even after my third miscarriage I searched for causes in my day-to-day activities. Had I lifted something heavy? Had I neglected nutrition or rest, even for a day? Had I been too anxious? Had I inhaled something toxic? I was always watchful; I even *wanted* to find something tangible to blame myself for. The actual finding wasn't crucial, though. I blamed myself even in the absence of any evidence.

And I let others—often well-meaning people—assign the blame to me, too. So many people spoke disapprovingly about my full-time job that I arranged to cut back to a three-day work week after the first miscarriage. When I made bread, someone would point out how much I was taking on: working, child care, home management, *even* baking my own bread! I was constantly advised to slow down, cut back, change my ways. The implication that my ways were deleterious to a pregnancy did not, of course, escape me. When I jogged, many rushed to point out that it had a jiggling effect on the fetus. So I stopped jogging. Kindly (I do not mean this sarcastically) people pointedly asked me if I "drank much" when I sipped a single glass of wine with dinner. I remember one older woman summing it up when she said:

> Sometimes I think that young girls these days are paying for the way they change the natural order of life around. They defer children until they are ready, and even then they go out to work during the pregnancies and after their babies are born. Don't they want to be with the infants? Maybe nature is protecting the babies!

For those of us who have any ambivalence about full-time mothering (and isn't that most of us?) her comments pack quite a wallop.

There's probably a bit of detective in each of us. Everyone wanted to solve the mystery. I am convinced that people were motivated by kindness, a desire to help, or a need to console me. I certainly was more eager than anyone to put an end to the speculation (mine and everyone else's), even if it meant taking on total, irrevocable responsibility for the miscarriages. What people obviously did not realize was that everyone's questions and suggestions became additional fuel for my guilt.

The fact that I was an habitual aborter (three consecutive miscarriages) makes my experience a little different from the experience of women who have had one or two miscarriages. I had more time to work out the complex, troubling emotional responses. Each new experience brought more intensity to the emotions. Interestingly though, almost every woman I talked with, whether or not she had had more than one miscarriage, described similar responses. Their experiences differed only in timing and intensity. Physical fear was a part of each woman's experience. The intensity of the fear seemed to relate not only to the physical changes going on in her body, but also to the level of understanding she had of those changes (from previous miscarriages, other women's descriptions, her physician's explanations). Lorraine told me:

> I can't even describe my sense of terror the first time I miscarried. I was watering the tomato plants we'd just put in—and when I looked down there was blood dripping near my feet. I could hardly believe it was coming from me. It happened so suddenly, and I bled a lot. I guess I instinctively knew I was losing the baby, I just panicked. I couldn't figure out what to do. It's a lucky thing Paul was there—he called the doctor and had me lie down and got us to the hospital—all without showing he was upset. I just really went to pieces. . . .

Ruth talked about her second miscarriage in less than a year:

> The second time I was a real trooper. I felt worse, emotionally, after it was over, but I handled the event itself with real class! Don was away on a business trip, and we'd just moved to the suburbs, so I didn't know anyone nearby. I even arranged a babysitter for Jennifer without mentioning where I was going. Luckily the Welcome Wagon people had just left me a list of sitters. The girl who came was very nice. I bet she had a heart attack later when my sister came back instead of me. I went to the doctor's office. He was just going to the hospital; he even gave me a ride! I called my sister at work just before they anesthetized me, and she handled the home front. I guess if I hadn't been bleeding so much, the doctor wouldn't have moved so fast on it. The contractions were so mild I could have gone on for days without much discomfort. My handling of the situation even surprised me. The first time I had been so scared I could hardly speak to the nurses. I guess my doctor's support and openness and the kindness of all

the hospital people erased my fears. I really wasn't afraid that second time, though I must admit I was a basket case afterwards, wondering whether I'd ever have more children.

Unfortunately most women have little information available to them when they abort. In spite of the high percentage of pregnancies that end in miscarriage every year, we don't seem to share our experiences with one another. Perhaps because miscarriage, unlike childbirth, is a sad and unrewarding event, we're hesitant to ask for or offer details. Another possible explanation lies in our society's general inability to cope with the subject of death. We do not usually have direct contact with death as earlier generations did. It occurs safely apart from our lives, in hospitals and nursing homes in most cases. This probably contributes to our difficulty in accepting and dealing with any form of death.

The disappointment and sadness I have described is also clearly a universal theme. Feeling sad and depressed for weeks or months after a miscarriage seems to be the norm. Many women say that they didn't get over their feelings of sadness until they were pregnant again. The reality of postpartum (after-childbirth) depression is often forgotten in this context. When we miscarry, our bodies' hormonal balances change as abruptly as they do after childbirth. Hence we are subject to as much chemically induced emotional disorder with none of the usual rewards. There's no baby, no happy visitors showering us with gifts and attention, no approval, no fun! Vicki described it this way:

After my miscarriage I was so depressed. I had wanted that baby so much! I just couldn't seem to snap out of it. Oh, people were nice. They tried to help—calling and saying cheerful things and "chin up, kid" and stuff like that—but nobody really wanted to talk about

it. When I wasn't responding well in a couple of
weeks, I noticed the calls tapered off. I felt like
I was failing everybody. I really wanted to be brave
and tough, but my sadness was overwhelming. Even
when I'd see someone handling an infant on TV
in some stupid baby-powder commercial, I'd break
down. . . .

Undoubtedly the strongest emotional response that most of
us have after a miscarriage is *guilt*. Without exception every
woman I talked with had experienced or *was still* experiencing feelings of guilt. Many reported the same "detective"
attitude that I have described. They continued to look back
for months after they miscarried, seeking a "probable cause"
in their own behavior just prior to the miscarriage. Lorraine
said:

I don't know if I'll ever stop feeling guilty about those
two miscarriages. Even now, six years and two children
later, I feel a rush of remorse when we talk about it.
Those were two babies I'd have loved like I love my
two boys now. My life-style during those two pregnancies was all wrong—working much too hard, eating
junk food, no sleep, et cetera. I was finishing my
doctorate, and really keyed up and anxious all the time.
I just shouldn't have gotten pregnant.

Like Lorraine, many women isolated certain factors and
identified them as causes of the miscarriage. Jane felt that
taking a three-mile walk in the cold on a day when she wasn't
feeling up to par had precipitated her first miscarriage, and
that her unsettled state (she and her husband were in the midst
of a move to another city) had precipitated her second
miscarriage.

Both times it had been a bad time for me to be pregnant. I just felt if only I could get the timing right and be very careful. I just felt I hadn't tried hard enough . . .

She prescribed her own course of therapy for the third pregnancy—three months' bed rest—and successfully carried to term a healthy boy. While her diagnosis and recommendations worked, she did feel guilty for both unsuccessful pregnancies.

Anita blamed her recent miscarriage on the frequency with which she and her husband had sexual relations during her early pregnancy.

My mother had told me that there are many things you shouldn't do until a pregnancy has had a chance to, uh, become secure. One of those things was sex. I kind of wrote off what she said as old-fashioned. The doctor hadn't said so . . . now I wish I'd listened. . . . She had six children, she ought to know. . . . Lou has agreed now that when I become pregnant again, we won't take any chances. . . .

It's not hard to imagine the added strains on a couple who are already under stress after they decide that their sexual activities were to blame for the miscarriage they suffered. The relationship between the man and woman suffers a great deal of damage if they don't correct that misunderstanding. Sex does not cause miscarriages, but feelings of guilt may nevertheless persist.

Other women with whom I talked even blamed themselves for the inadequate medical care they had received. Mary had been leaking what she thought might be amniotic fluid for several days. When she called her obstetrician, he reassured her that "extra discharge was normal." She miscarried two weeks later, in her fifth month. Mary still feels "rotten that I didn't press him to see me and examine me as soon as I noticed it. . . . Who knows, maybe he'd have been able to do something. . . ."

Barbara, who became pregnant while she had an IUD in her uterus, wanted the IUD removed or an abortion performed because of her fears of harming the fetus. Her doctor convinced her that her fears were unwarranted and advised her to continue the pregnancy. (Although doctors would now remove the IUD as soon as a woman is found to be pregnant.) She miscarried in her sixth month, suffering a great deal of mental anguish as well as a very difficult physical recovery. Barbara still blames herself for not having sought a second opinion or pressing her own stand against her doctor's.

> All the women I told urged me to have it removed —my sister, my cousin, friends, Frank's mother. And my gut feeling was that it wasn't safe. . . . I don't know why I let him talk me into leaving it. It's the stupidest thing I've ever done. I think it all boils down to me being a nice girl and doing what I'm told . . . by the most impressive authority . . . The whole experience was so traumatic, I don't know if I'll ever get over it. . . .

Most of the women with whom I talked felt that discussing their miscarriages with outsiders only made them feel guiltier. Some chose not to talk about their miscarriages with anyone other than their mate because they didn't find other people's suggestions or questions helpful. Again this problem is one of lack of information, or misinformation. People do not realize that the largest percentage of miscarriages probably occur as a result of genetic accident, over which we have *no* control. But with the scientific uncertainty that exists, the situation lends itself to the home-remedy approach. Because the next try (after a miscarriage) is usually successful, people may conclude that there was some efficacy in whatever behavioral change was recommended.

There is another common experience that both men and women may have to a miscarriage. It is called by some the survival syndrome. This is a sense of relief that follows the stress of the miscarriage. It is a peaceful, almost happy moment when you realize that you have *survived* and will be able to live, love, and try again to have a family.

The survival syndrome is only one step in the entire process of adjusting to a spontaneous abortion. You should realize that it is normal to feel anger and frustration as well as relief. You and your loved ones should not be surprised if after the period of relief you find yourself once again depressed, angry, melancholy, or sad. It is an unusual person who can accept misfortune without a reasonable period of mourning.

For some the period of adjustment goes on for many years, while for others it is much shorter. There is no right or wrong interval after which you should have adjusted to your emotional feelings. All of us are different in this respect. About the best you can do is to be open to your needs and the needs of those close to you. If you need help from outside professionals, we suggest that you seek it openly. Good counseling can help you air issues that you might not be able to resolve with your loved ones or by yourself.

I've tried to talk here about some of the emotions that I and other women I interviewed felt when we faced miscarriages. It's quite evident that patterns and commonalities exist among us. In fact, it is these very commonalities that have proven most supportive to some of us. In a similar sense, we reach out for support in much the same direction, toward husbands, families, friends, physicians, and others.

SUMMARY

1. The emotional aspect of the miscarriage experience is probably the most difficult.
2. Many of us have similar emotional responses to a miscarriage.
3. Some immediate reactions include fear, anger, and disappointment.
4. Some of us begin to view ourselves differently, as powerless, unfortunate failures.
5. Guilt, self-imposed as well as the variety dispensed by well-meaning friends and relatives, is very often a big problem.
6. Many of us take on responsibility for factors that are completely beyond our control (e.g. inadequate medical care).
7. Unfortunately most women have little experience with or knowledge of miscarriage prior to their own miscarriages; information on this topic does not seem to be shared readily.

IX

The Man's Emotions

Although a miscarriage is an event that happens to both the man and the woman, his feelings are often lost in the bustle of doctor, hospital, and recuperation which focuses on the woman. This is unfortunate for both of them, since his feelings are likely to be intense and will need to have appropriate outlets.

THE HOSPITAL EXPERIENCE

The initial medical crisis is hers. During that time the man must take on a secondary role, acting as the woman's helper, protector, and advocate in the hospital. Centuries of tradition have left men fairly comfortable with the protector role, though dealing with the medical establishment in this capacity is often very difficult. You may not understand the technical language or how the system works. This is likely to make you feel helpless and left out at this stage, and you may feel uncertain of how to behave during the events that follow.

It is also difficult for many men to show their emotions openly in front of strangers. Since most institutions are not set up with private areas for the man and woman to talk to each other, it may feel awkward for him to cry or display other strong emotions that are sometimes considered unmanly. This is unfortunate, because it sets the two of them apart and may make him feel self-conscious.

Paul recounted his feelings about the hospital in this way. He had wanted the baby, yet was uncertain about what to say to Lorraine when she came out of the anesthesia.

> When Lorraine started bleeding, I was very scared. It came on suddenly, and she bled a lot. I don't think I gave much thought to the baby during that time. I was just worried about her. Before I could even reach the doctor on the phone she was having bad cramps or contractions.
>
> He said that he'd meet us at the hospital. I don't think I'd ever seen her in pain before in five years of marriage. It was awful. I stayed with her until she was anesthetized, holding her hand and trying to be calm.
>
> It wasn't until she was back in the room after the D and C that I was able to think ahead. I felt bad. We'd both really wanted this baby and had been trying for nearly a year before she became pregnant. I knew she'd be wrecked when she came to, and I realized that I didn't have any idea what to say. I kept thinking . . . I don't ever want to put her through this again.

Paul's thoughts are common to many men. There is an uncertainty about what to do and say, mixed with a deep feeling of powerlessness and helplessness when you see the person you love in pain. His reaction—"I don't ever want to put her through this again''—assumed the blame for the spontaneous abortion was his. This guilt feeling does not acknowledge that they *both* wanted the baby. The miscarriage affects both partners; it is not anyone's fault.

Don expressed other feelings about the hospital that are true for many men:

> You'll probably think this is terrible, but I was kind of glad that I was away when Ruth miscarried this last time. She managed so well, with her sister and also the help of her doctor. I didn't even know about it till it was over.
>
> The first miscarriage was the worst thing I've ever been through. She was terrified and wouldn't let go of my hand. I had to pull it away from her when they asked me to leave the room. And she cried so much. Ruth is not a crier, so I'm not used to it like some men. And to be honest with you, I'm really afraid of hospitals. The only times I've been in them have been when my parents died and when our daughter was born. Even then I was out in the waiting room. I don't like the sight of blood. It makes me sick. When she had that first miscarriage, I had to force myself to stay with her. I kept wanting to bolt.

For many men a spontaneous abortion may be their first direct contact with a medical emergency and with the hospital setting. Often this happens to young couples, and men rarely see doctors for their own care until middle age. Hence the strangeness of the situation makes it more difficult to respond appropriately to their mates.

Tom's situation was a bit different, but it still demonstrates how hard it is to be with your loved one when she is suffering. He was a medical student at the time his wife, Vicki, miscarried. Moreover he had worked as an orderly in a hospital emergency room during college, so he had been exposed to medical emergencies. But when it was Vicki who was going through the miscarriage, he still felt helpless and somewhat overcome by the situation.

> I had seen all kinds of emergencies with plenty of blood and guts and emotion—but never with anyone close to me. I felt completely powerless and wasted. Vicki was terribly upset and having a lot of pain, too. I wanted to rescue her or take away the pain, and I couldn't do a damn thing except watch her cry.

Though men may feel useless in this situation they should be very aware of how important their presence is. It is something that happens to both of you, and your presence reinforces this. By being in the hospital and expressing your own fear and grief, you share the experience with her. It can give both of you added strength. You are a support person among many strange faces—an intermediary in an institutional setting that can be very frightening.

It is unfortunate that the hospital setting is so difficult and alienating for men, because this strangeness may further delay their opportunity to express their own feelings. They should be aware that the awkwardness they feel is quite common and will probably pass when the man and woman go home together. However just being there with your mate will be important to both of you later on.

ADJUSTING TO YOUR LOSS

Once the medical crisis has passed, the man's role becomes more important, and his feelings become more apparent. He, too, has suffered a loss, and both man and woman should share the pain and disappointment. In this way they can provide each other with emotional support. Men should expect that it is *normal* to feel many intense emotions from the miscarriage experience. It is common to feel *sadness, disbelief, anger, frustration*, and even *pessimism* about their future ability to have children.

Often the initial response to a loss is *disbelief*. It may be hard to fully appreciate the fact that the spontaneous abortion has really happened to you, since just a short time before you and your family were preparing to welcome a new baby. This period of disbelief is characterized by a numbness or haziness. Many aspects of life will seem far away, as if they were happening to someone else. It may seem like a bad dream which you wish you could wake up from and bring to an end. Pete described his experience quite well in this regard:

> Mary had no pain or contractions with the miscarriage. She just noticed some spotting one day, and when she saw her doctor the pregnancy test was negative. He scheduled her for a D and C because it seemed like she wasn't going to pass the fetus.
>
> So the next day we went to the hospital and checked in. I could've easily been in Toledo. I was detached from it, and there really wasn't anything for me to do. But I went with her and sat in the waiting room. She had a local anesthetic so I didn't even have to see her unconscious. I guess we were both kind of numb through the whole thing, hardly crying or showing emotion. It wasn't until weeks later that we realized how depressed we both were and how empty.

After the period of disbelief passes (and it may take hours, days, or weeks—everyone is different), feelings of anger and frustration are likely to surface. "Why me?" is a common reaction. "Other people have all the children they want, why can't we?'' So along with the feeling of sadness is the feeling of anger.

Unfortunately these angry feelings are all too easily displaced onto the people who are closest to us. Men have a tendency to *blame* their mates or to blame themselves for something that they did during the pregnancy. Men do not carry the pregnancy, so it is easy to put the responsibility onto the other person. And few men understand that it is their genetic system that might have caused the problem. While this response is a common one, it is extremely damaging to the relationship. We rarely know why a given couple aborts, and every effort must be made to avoid blaming the other person.

For some the significance of the spontaneous abortion will depend on their investment in being a father. To some men this is a central theme in life and part of their family and social tradition. These complex cultural norms shape our values and perceptions. When they are frustrated, many emotions are aroused including sadness and anger. As one physician commented:

> I see many men who become quite angry with their wives after the miscarriage. For some men there is a real ethnic feeling about having children. It is part of their whole cultural background, and for them it may be a disaster. Their goal in life is to be a father and to be part of a family. Sometimes we [doctors] are not enough part of their culture to be a help to them.

Some men may also harbor *guilty* feelings within themselves. They may assign responsibility for the miscarriage to themselves, particularly if they believe that sexual intercourse caused the miscarriage in some way. As Dr. Henry Klapholz explained:

The husbands are frequently guilty about intercourse. That is a very common feeling, and they have to be reassured that that wasn't the case, and that there was nothing that they did to cause this.

I had a couple recently who were using contraception even though their religion forbade it. They had had six children and got pregnant due to the failure of the diaphragm. They felt very guilty now that she was miscarrying, because they had used contraception, and felt that it had somehow fouled up the embryo.

Men should participate in the medical investigation for the cause of the spontaneous abortion. Once they know that they have not passed on a genetic abnormality or genitourinary infection that might be causing the miscarriage, they should try to put these guilt feelings aside.

Whether the desire to have a family and take on the father's role is based on family tradition, culture, or personal expectations is not particularly important to our discussion. What is important is that a miscarriage, like any other important loss in life, will provoke strong emotional responses. It is natural for men to go through much of the same emotional turmoil that women do, and to go through a period of adjustment followed by periods of sadness, anger, frustration, or other unpleasant feelings. There is nothing unmasculine about this, and they should allow themselves the time and space to go through this normal process of adjusting. Grieving takes time and is painful for everyone involved. Men should be able to admit that they have sustained a loss of great magnitude and not feel that they have to hide their feelings.

John described his reaction this way:

Betty and I had planned this pregnancy for about two years. We had waited to have a child until both of us were out of school and making some money. Being a parent is something that I had always wanted, and I felt empty after the miscarriage. It was like a dream had died. Something that I had already considered to be ours was never going to be realized. I think that it wasn't until the next pregnancy that I stopped being sad about the miscarriage.

EXPRESSING YOURSELF

Even though men feel all of these emotions, they may find it difficult to express them. Some of the difficulty arises from cultural attitudes that associate emotionality with weakness. Many men feel that it is inappropriate for a man to express sadness openly. However, some of a man's reluctance to express oneself may have to do with his desire to be strong and comforting for his mate. Peter recounted this to us:

> There was a kind of paradox that happened after the miscarriage. I was hurt and depressed, but I didn't want to show it to the extent that I thought it would make it harder for Amy. I thought that she would want me to be strong in the face of her suffering.
> And I also felt that someone had to take care of our lives. Someone had to work, take care of the house, and keep things going while she was going through her difficult times.

However, denying your feelings or keeping them from your mate may become a problem for *both* of you. She may feel that you are insensitive and do not feel the same sense of loss that she does. In addition she may interpret your outward self-control as an expression of masculine superiority. It is true that your feelings may not seem to be as intense as your partner's, but if you share her grief, it is best to share it openly. You may both find more strength in this than if one of you merely keeps up the facade of strength and leaves the other to grieve alone. Sharing feelings can give you both a sense of equality as partners.

Here are two stories that illustrate the problems that arise when the man and woman express their grief differently:

> I thought that things were going pretty well. We were both back to our normal activities in a week or so. I felt sad, but I guess what I did was put it out of my mind. When I saw her getting down, I tried to provide some entertainment, diversion—you know. Then—I think it was two or three weeks after the miscarriage—Jane blew up one night, accusing me of being uncaring and insensitive. She said it was obvious I hadn't been hurt by the loss of the baby.
>
> I was shocked. I'd thought that the least I could do was to act cheerful and positive, and not get her down. It turned out she had wanted me to show her that I was hurting, too. At first I felt angry. Here I'd been walking on eggs trying to preserve her equilibrium, trying to take care of her, and she's accusing me of insensitivity.
>
> But the more we talked about it, the more I understood. It's not my way to talk about things that are sad, but this is my wife, and we did have a big disappointment together. I think if I were in the situation again—and I hope to God I'm not—I'd probably let down a lot more to Jane. She said it would have helped her to know that I was feeling a lot of the same stuff. That makes sense to me now.

Bill told us about his relationship with Alice:

> To tell you the truth, Alice and I never discussed it after the first few days. Her friend spent a lot of time with

her, and they seemed to be always talking about it. I
thought it was best to leave well enough alone. I did try
to be extra gentle and affectionate with her, and I'd
have to say I put up with more than my share of
bullshit, because she was so edgy and emotional for a
while.

When she got pregnant again I was very nervous for
the first few months, but I didn't say anything to her. I
certainly didn't want to make her nervous, and she
seemed really happy.

When this came up and we talked about your in-
terviewing us, she said how nervous she had been in
that pregnancy. Strange, huh? That was the first I knew
that she was worried. You live together, and you sleep
together, and you'd do anything for this person, but
sometimes you have no idea what is going on in her
head.

Don spoke of the kind of estrangement and anger that can
arise from a failure to communicate:

I think that I paid my dues by the time it was all over.
I'd been relieved, as I said, to have missed the second
miscarriage. But her reaction afterwards was much worse
than after the first one. When I'd come home, she'd be
crying, every night for weeks. She'd bring Jennifer, our
three-year-old, to me and go in the bedroom and cry
herself to sleep.

It was murder. I thought I'd go crazy. Sometimes I'd
go in and sit with her and try to find out what was
wrong. Sometimes I'd take Jen and go for a ride and
bring Ruth an ice cream or something. Nothing worked.
The first time she had been in rough shape for a week,
but it got better after that. When she had the second
miscarriage, of course, she started thinking she was in

real trouble and there wouldn't be any more kids. Finally we went to the obstetrician together, at my request, and talked to him—a kind of counseling session. He's really a great guy. I couldn't tell you exactly what he said, but things started to improve afterwards. It was gradual, but it did get better.

Robert related a similar story:

For the first few weeks after the miscarriage I did everything I could to cheer Linda up. I tried to plan little treats, outings, surprises. I tried so hard to be good that it probably seemed phony. It wasn't until I let out some of my own fears that we began to talk seriously about ourselves and about our future for having children. Thinking about it, I probably resented having to be so cheerful.

Robert and Don attempted to hide their feelings so that they would provide strength for their loved ones. In both situations it proved to be better to express their own grief and allow their partners the opportunity to relate to those feelings. Many women prefer this. There is a difference between being cheerful and providing comfort. Comforting each other can validate the perfectly appropriate emotions that you are sharing.

The point we are trying to make is that you should express whatever you feel. Be open to each other and get whatever strength you can from the feelings you share as a couple. If you feel depressed, that is an acceptable feeling for a man. If you have ambivalent feelings about fatherhood or trying to have a family together, it is important for you to deal with them. We have come to a time when it is entirely appropriate for men to express emotion, just as it is for women.

SEEING THINGS DIFFERENTLY

Once you do get involved with each other's feelings, you should expect that there will be times when you see things differently. Great personal crises like a spontaneous abortion can bring out other problems that are occurring in the relationship.

It is important to try to keep the various emotional issues separate. If you are just using the issue of the miscarriage as a pretext for renewing some earlier conflict, you will be doing yourselves a disservice. When you seem to be fighting about everything all at once, this is a signal to seek professional counseling. In such an instance the problems go beyond the miscarriage, and you are just using that as an excuse to hurt each other.

It is hard to give men specific strategies for dealing with sadness. For some men it is difficult to express sadness openly, and even knowing that this will separate them from their partners will not make it easier. Both men and women need to be patient if this happens and allow for each other's ways of expressing their feelings. There is a natural tendency to become frustrated in the face of these differences.

In some places there are men's groups where men can discuss these issues. They provide a forum for men to talk about their lives and seek common solutions. In some cities there are even groups where men meet to talk specifically about pregnancy and parenting. It is hoped that this service will spread to more places so that more men can support each other in times of stress. Just as women often gain important emotional strength from one another, men do also. Discussion is an important outlet for both men and women.

Above all try to understand that most people need a period of grieving. Sometimes men forget this and rush back to work to try to avoid their pain and frustration. If you do not give yourself a chance to sort out your feelings, they are likely to remain trapped inside you, and may come out in negative ways.

We have found that though there are differences in the ways men and women feel and express themselves, these differences are certainly not so great that they prevent them from understanding each other if they make the effort. Most women seem to want to talk with their men about what has happened. They want to share their sadness aloud and to be assured of their mate's love. They want to relieve their guilt feelings and talk about the future of the relationship. Men want this, too, but often find it difficult to initiate the talk. However, it needs to be done. You will probably find that once you do talk, there is a lot you share. Your response to this unfortunate event can strengthen your relationship.

Jeff summed this up pretty well:

> When Megan miscarried, I felt terrible. I just kept on thinking and hoping that we would make it through together, that we would be able to have the next pregnancy work. Now that it's been a year since that happened, I see that we learned from it. We grew closer from it. We suffered together and cried. She kept on saying that nothing comes easily in life, and that the next time would be different. I came to see a lot of strength in her that I hadn't seen before. I think she saw a lot of love in me that maybe she hadn't seen before, either.

SUMMARY

1. The events in the hospital are very difficult for men. They often feel powerless and frustrated at a time when they want very much to help their loved ones.

2. Men should accept that it is normal to feel many intense emotions after the miscarriage, including disbelief, sadness, anger, frustration, and guilt.

3. Adjusting to the loss that accompanies a spontaneous abortion takes time. It is acceptable for men to feel the emotional effects of the abortion for weeks and months afterwards. There is a common series of events that people go through in the grieving process, and this does not often happen quickly.

4. Men often blame their mate for the miscarriage. This has no basis in scientific fact and is likely to be very dangerous for the relationship.

5. Guilt feelings may arise after the miscarriage, especially about sexual relations during pregnancy. There is no scientific evidence that links sexual intercourse or any kind of lovemaking with spontaneous abortions.

6. Differences in the ways men and women express their emotions may cause tension in the relationship. It is important for men to be open about their feelings, so that their mates understand that they too have suffered a loss.

7. If you find that you are fighting about many things with your mate, it is time to seek professional counseling. Avoid allowing the issue of the spontaneous abortion to become the focus for all the problems in your relationship.

X

The Reactions
of Others

The man usually acts as the woman's primary source of emotional support. In most cases he's the second-most involved person. He's there (or called) when the emergency begins. It's his loss as well. Most significantly, he's there to live through the aftereffects. Nevertheless, there are other people who can play important roles in helping the woman through this difficult time.

Many of the women I talked with spoke of drawing their greatest support from women friends. Women certainly empathize more easily with what have been called "women's troubles." They've had cramps or, perhaps, given birth. They usually know more about pregnancy, labor, and delivery. More important, they know or can readily understand how many complex feelings are involved in the desire to be a mother. Alice told me:

> I don't know how I'd have gotten through the experience if it hadn't been for my friend Kim. Although

she lives on the other side of the city, she was there every day for the whole week after I got out of the hospital. She just brought her little girl with some toys to play with, settled her in the living room, and made lunch for me and sat talking with me for most of the afternoon. The first few days I was pretty weepy and so was she. . . . I really knew she knew what I was going through. She also straightened out the house and a couple of times left dinner so Ron wouldn't have to do it when he got home. I know Ron did his best, but it was those afternoons with Kim that held my head together.

My mother talked about her sisters' taking turns staying with her, caring for the house and her three children:

If they hadn't been able to come in and do all that for me, I wouldn't have had any recovery time. Dad couldn't stay home from work for more than a day or two, and you kids were too young to take care of yourselves or anything else. I surely did feel sad and let down, but the feeling of exhaustion was the largest one I remember. Being able to sleep and rest in bed as much as I needed to was the biggest luxury I could have asked for. They knew that—even though they hadn't had children themselves—and, of course, they sympathized and knew how I was feeling and did extra little things for me, too—little gifts, my favorite foods. . . .

Some women, like me, were fortunate enough to have friends around who had had miscarriages themselves. There's no substitute for having been there. Hearing someone else's account of her physical experiences can go a long way toward alleviating the fears of a woman who is still in the process of miscarrying or who has just been confronted with a diagnosis of "threatened abortion." Similarly it can be soothing to know that someone else has gone through what you have gone through and succeeded some months or years later in having a normal pregnancy.

Sharing the emotional aspects of the experience with someone who had felt it all too was as important. I felt at many times that I was being weak or overreacting when weeks later I still wasn't "in charge" emotionally. Hearing someone else describe the same behavior patterns somehow validated those emotions. Ruth described herself as a "basket case" after her second miscarriage:

> For several weeks after the second one I was in really tough shape. I could get by most of the day taking care of Jennifer, going to the park, play group, even keeping up with housework. But as soon as Don came home and I could go off duty, I'd start crying. I just couldn't seem to control the crying. I knew he thought I was overreacting. I even thought so! But I couldn't get in control . . . for quite a while. . . .

During our interview Ruth expressed relief and happiness when she heard that I, too, and many other women I'd talked with had gone through weeks like this.

When I had my third miscarriage, a friend with whom I had been spending a great deal of time suffered a miscarriage within days of mine. Amazing and shocking as that was for both of us, I think in certain ways that it pulled us both through. By then I had a history of miscarriages, but Susan didn't. That was the only major sense in which our experiences varied. Having someone with whom to share and compare, blow by blow, the details of what we were going through during the week that preceded our D and C's really did make it more bearable. We didn't have to spare each other the gory details or deal with each other's sympathy or pity. We were both miserable and anxious yet somehow helpful to each other. That was a freak incident, of course, but it further reinforced for me the awareness of the need we have for communication on this subject.

Most of the women I spoke with talked about contact with their mothers in the course or aftermath of their miscarriages. In my case that was particularly helpful, since my mother had experienced multiple miscarriage herself. Twice she came to take care of me and help run the house. For the second miscarriage she was there for several days preceding the D and C while I was bleeding and still hoping to salvage the pregnancy. Her presence was immensely comforting in itself because she is that kind of person. The additional bonus for me was that she could talk or listen all day on that one subject. We talked pretty constantly about miscarriages—mine, hers, those of friends of hers. Her generation of women, maybe because they were having more pregnancies, seemed to be very much more aware of one another's miscarriages and involved in one another's recoveries. There was obviously less mystery and fear in it for them. The more stories I heard, the less freakish I felt and the more hopeful that I might someday succeed at this pregnancy business.

The mother-child bonding that is present in this situation is pretty undeniable, too. Who better can empathize with your need for mothering, in both meanings of the word, than the one who had to mother you? Women who have reasonably good relationships with their mothers can draw great support from this direction. Vicki felt that sharing her experiences with her mother strengthened a less than satisfactory relationship:

> When Tom suggested we call my mother and ask her to come and stay a few days to help me, I was very hesitant. She and I had never gotten along very well. I'd always felt that I wasn't the kind of daughter she'd

had in mind; in fact, when my brother married, Mom and my sister-in-law immediately became close. I think Mom was finding the daughterlike companionship there. It sounds like I was jealous—I guess I was. Anyway Tom really pressed the issue, since he works long hours and knew he wouldn't have time off to be with me. I was surprised and pleased to find that she and I got along wonderfully. We talked about childbirth and family life. I told her about the miscarriage—she'd never had one and didn't know what happens in your body. All in all it was an enriching experience for me in spite of my depression. We've been much closer since then. . . .

The essential quality here is not the words that are said or the particular style of mothering but the nurturing relationship.

For those of us who already have a child or children when we miscarry, we have still another very important relationship to consider. A child in a family that is suffering a miscarriage is certainly aware that some important event is taking place. This can be very upsetting if the parents do not take the time to explain what is going on; children's imaginations can make matters far more frightening than the reality would be. The emotional upheaval in the home, combined with the "illness" and/or hospitalization of the mother, has a tremendous impact on the child.

Guilt may be another complicating factor. Although most children anticipate the birth of a sibling with rather unrealistic joy, some do not. For the child who has expressed his distaste for the idea of having a sibling or perhaps secretly wished there would not be another baby, there can be serious guilt problems. Young children have a tendency to blame themselves for all kinds of events that occur in their environments. As parents it is necessary for us to explain clearly and repeatedly that the loss of the baby had nothing to do with them. This is essential even if the child has asked no questions and has given no other evidence that she or he feels guilty, because those feelings often are so troubling to youngsters that they are pushed down to levels well below the surface.

My daughter, Suze, was four years old when I had my first miscarriage. She had known about the pregnancy and had been excited in her four-year-old way about the brother or sister who was in her future. Talking about the miscarriage was painful to me, but we did share our sadness and tears much more readily than I could with most adults. Mark and I explained to her that the baby had stopped growing because of some physical problem over which we had no control and that some time in the future we hoped another baby would grow successfully.

In the next two pregnancies we were more careful about exciting her too early. Consequently, when the miscarriages occurred, she was not even aware that I was pregnant. Her emotional response when we explained my "illnesses" and hospitalizations was less intense. This more secretive method of handling the two later pregnancies was effective for us because she was so young and because we were equally slow in announcing our news to other people. With older children I would not recommend it because of the danger of an information leak. Different families obviously handle the dissemination of private family information in different ways. The explanation will certainly depend on the age and interest-level of the children. It is essential, however, to recognize the children's sensitivity to what is happening in their environments and their right to honest and understandable explanations.

We made a real effort to provide just such an explanation, and we were surprised when Suze asked sometime after the second miscarriage, "Did that baby decide to start growing again yet, Mom?" I took pains to show her with illustrations the whole process of sperm, egg, implantation, uterine lining, etc. We stressed the fact that the baby was gone—did not "work." We restated our hope that *another* baby would be conceived and grow and "work"—but that it would not be a slow or stubborn grower. A month or two later she asked the same question again.

Especially at times like these, with a subject that is painful to discuss, it is easy for us to forget the child's need for repetition. Children need these explanations and clarifications many times. They forget, or they may absorb only part of the information we give them. In some cases they are afraid to ask questions because of the parents' obvious distress. For these reasons it is very important for parents to return to the subject periodically, listening carefully to make sure that the child is clear about what the events were, what caused those events, and what to expect in the future.

I guess that in some ways Suze became even more precious to me with each pregnancy that did not succeed. I draw a lot from her under any circumstances. After the miscarriages, such painful and anxious times, her unconditional love and devotion were particularly comforting. The women I spoke with who already had children when they miscarried all alluded to the tendency to turn in—towards their families and children—for a while afterwards. The parents' resources are particularly diminished after a miscarriage. I am convinced, however, that helping the child to deal with her or his emotions can help us face our own. Perhaps this dynamic is one of the hidden bonuses of parenting.

Another important resource is the physician. Most of us rely pretty heavily on the opinions and suggestions of our doctors as well as on their medical expertise. They tend to be the ones who tell us what's going on in our bodies (and if we already know, they validate our knowledge). They certainly are the ones who explain the medical facts of the situation. Unfortunately in many cases they do not choose or are not able to deal with the emotional component of the miscarriage. Physicians have the opportunity to heal the *whole* woman, mind and body, primarily because most of us invest so much faith and confidence in them. This attention to the whole person is all too often lacking. Limitations of time, training, and in some cases sensitivity work against us.

When I remarked about this to Dr. Fred Storm, the obstetrician who has helped me through these past few years, he urged me to be understanding of his colleagues' limitations:

> Don't forget that it's only recently that medical students have been getting any training in this part of medicine. In the past the closest we got to it was our psychiatry classes and rotations through psych sections in the third or fourth year. Those were deviant populations—I don't remember anyone speaking to the emotional needs of the normal populations we'd be treating. . . . So most of us in practice have worked from our own instincts, our own personalities. Some people are more compassionate, or more able to convey compassion and warmth, than others. Some doctors, like many people, can't deal with emotion very well. . . . Sometimes they ignore it, which is unfortunate for both the patient and the doctor. . . . I guess I do the best I can to show the patient that I care, but sometimes I'm really dissatisfied with the words that come out. . . .

One experience with a rather cold obstetrician who examined me at the time of my first miscarriage convinced me that I could not risk being in the care of such an individual again. After that I was careful to see that the physician who cared for my pregnancies was able to relate to the affective side of me as his patient as well as the physical side.

I was lucky to have found him. Office visits were interesting and unrushed; he believes very strongly in educating his patients. He spent time talking with me after each miscarriage about my potential for future pregnancies, as well as about the probable cause of the miscarriage. At the time of the D and C's he was kind, sympathetic, and available. He answered all my questions honestly and shared all the decision-making with both Mark and me. More than once he held my hand and talked to me as I went under the sodium pentothal. When I saw him in the office a few weeks later he talked with me again, always unrushed, solicitous, and comforting. In short I felt he was really there for me. I trusted him and felt somewhat dependent, but not demeaned, in my relationship with him. My interviews with other women who have experienced miscarriages have convinced me that my case is exceptional. Perhaps this has something to do with the physician's concept of his specialty. When we talked about his field, Fred Storm said:

> You know, obstetrics and gynecology has traditionally been considered a surgical subspecialty, and I really think that it's much more than that. The surgical mentality is not one that is geared to handling other aspects of a patient's well-being. I've never considered myself exclusively a surgeon. I see myself more in the nature of a primary-care physician, and I think it's important for us to be prepared to render counseling-type care. . . .

I am most grateful to Dr. Fred Storm, but certainly sorry that the empathy and support I received from him is not universally available to the women who need it. My hope is that this situation is changing as the training our doctors receive changes, and, more important, as we become better medical consumers and seek the full range of care we really need.

All of the individuals I've talked about in this chapter are important resource people for the woman who has suffered a miscarriage. For reasons of temperament, conditioning, or circumstance, some are more able to help than others. The same elements may qualify our abilities to *seek* the help we need. It's crucial to recognize all the potential roadblocks and find the emotional support we need, whether it comes from the traditional sources or not.

SUMMARY

1. Men seem to experience the loss differently in a miscarriage. This can be stressful for the woman. Communicating as clearly and honestly as possible is probably the couple's most important task.
2. Women friends, especially those with personal experience of miscarriage, are often major sources of support. Sharing the physical as well as the emotional details seems to validate some of the emotions, as well as remove some of the mystery.
3. Many of us find great help and comfort in our own mothers. In many cases we are able to be taken care of by them in ways that we couldn't be by anyone else.
4. In families that already have children at the time of the miscarriage explaining the condition of the mother is essential. Children are aware, if only intuitively, that some disturbing event has occurred and deserve some clarification appropriate to their ages. Additionally, sharing the experience with the *whole* family can be more supportive to the grieving parents.

5. The physician who cares for us medically can be a very important source of advice, information, and emotional support as well. It's important to select someone who can deal with the emotional as well as the clinical aspects of the miscarriage.

XI

Normal Pregnancy After Miscarriage

After each miscarriage experience I became more and more concerned about my own activities during pregnancy. I had no idea why I had aborted, so my inclination was to be suspicious of all kinds of things. For instance I cut back on my work schedule, something which I had never contemplated doing prior to miscarrying. In my first pregnancy with Suze I had worked until the very end and felt good about it.

When the T-strain mycoplasma was found in my uterus, I finally had something concrete as a potential cause of my repeated abortions. Even after it seemed likely that this would no longer pose a problem, I was still concerned about exercise, diet, environment, work, and everything else that happened to my body during pregnancy. Each previous miscarriage had made my fears about the next pregnancy more intense. For that reason I became interested in learning about the proper maintenance of pregnancy. I wanted to maximize my chances of successfully carrying a normal, full-term child the next time.

OBSTETRIC CARE

Even before the miscarriages I had focused on the importance of choosing the right obstetrician, and this became increasingly important afterward. The medical aspects of my situation were very frightening to me. Then, more than ever before, I needed a warm, reassuring, unhurried physician.

I had researched the field very thoroughly before I even made an appointment, asking all the women I came in contact with for recommendations. Since I was fortunate enough to have a family connection with medicine in the city we lived in, I pursued information that way also. Mark and several of our friends had trained in the hospital where the local obstetricians practiced; their observations were invaluable. I also made a point of contacting the childbirth education programs in the area and asking for recommendations. The nurses I spoke with were very helpful in sharing feedback they had received from their students.

I finally did settle on one obstetrician and was ultimately quite satisfied. I think much of my good fortune in this regard had to do with my diligence in the search process and in my ability to verbalize what I wanted from the relationship *before* I became his patient.

The doctor we chose had a number of partners, but he was willing to be personally responsible for my care. This was essential to me, since I had no relationship with any of his partners and didn't want to begin one at a time of stress. Some doctors who practice in groups are not willing to commit themselves to this kind of arrangement; it is certainly not a convenient one for them. It is very important to be clear about this issue and others that are important to you in the doctor-patient relationship. If you fail to clarify things at the outset, you risk disappointment and anger later.

There were good reasons for my concern about the personal aspects of my treatment. I had had my share of five-minute gynecological visits. I'd also hesitated to "waste" doctors' time with questions or worries of mine in the past, and was finally determined to be a better consumer and a more satisfied patient.

The more I learned about spontaneous abortion, the more I realized that there was not much of a medical nature that the physician could do for my problem. Current medical knowledge is largely lacking in this area, and most adequately trained physicians know the proper tests to investigate the problem. There wasn't going to be any one person who would have a magical answer, drug, or operation of which his colleagues were unaware. So it wasn't so much what the person was going to *do*, but how he was going to interact with me that would be important. The doctor's care probably was not going to change the outcome of my pregnancy, but it would have a lot to do with how I felt about the experience.

I wanted the doctor to *care* about the emotional aspects of pregnancy and miscarriage. I also wanted him to let Mark be involved in our doctor-patient relationship and be present at the birth if my next pregnancy went to term.

To get these things, I had to do some shopping around and be clear about *my* requirements. I tried to sift through some basic data by phone when I called for an appointment. Questions that the phone staff wouldn't answer and points I wanted to discuss with the doctor I wrote down and checked off during my initial office visit. This visit is much like an audition, and it is natural to feel a certain amount of embarrassment or self-consciousness—but it is also important to overcome these feelings. We wouldn't dream of hiring other professionals, however specialized, without discussing the work involved. I think doctors need to be selected with equal care.

The issue of fees was important to me, as it is to everyone. I made a point of finding out before the relationship began what the doctor's fee schedule was. It wasn't too hard to do that over the phone, at least until my first miscarriage. Then I needed to find out what tests the physician would order, what would be covered by our insurance, how many visits would be involved, etc. Of course I discussed the costs of delivery as well. I didn't want to have one doctor treat my miscarriage problem and another deliver the baby. I learned from my comparison shopping that doctors' fees differ, sometimes dramatically, and paying more does not always mean that you get better care.

In addition I was looking for an intermediary to stand between me and the hospital. Mark and I knew well how hospitals are run and wanted our doctor to be our advocate there. That meant knowing what to expect before going in for any procedure. It also meant that I could rely on my physician, rather than interns, residents, or other house staff to make the decisions about my treatment.

I was thoroughly satisfied with the care that I received. In fact I like my doctor very much and feel that we were treated competently, kindly, and fairly. I believe that a major portion of my subsequent positive feelings was based on the fact that I was so careful in the beginning. I spelled out exactly what I wanted from the relationship in an assertive, open, and friendly way right from the beginning. During all of my pregnancies, and especially during my miscarriages, I kept attuned to my needs and spoke freely to our doctor. I feel that my active participation in my health care was as important in achieving our positive relationship as the competence and warmth of the physician. This was something that depended on both of us.

NUTRITION DURING PREGNANCY

No direct link between miscarriage and nutrition has ever been demonstrated. But a healthy pregnancy and having a healthy baby do depend on what you eat. So I was careful about my diet, hoping in the end that it would be an extra advantage if my next pregnancy was successful. My friend Pattie echoed my feelings when she told me:

> I don't know why I've had these miscarriages. I've never had anyone tell me that there is something wrong with Bill or me, but I am still conscious of everything I do that may affect my staying pregnant. I don't know the effect of the air I breathe in the city, drinking the water, or even riding in a car. What I know I can control most easily is what I eat. That goes into both of us, you know, me and the baby.

Maintaining a proper diet during pregnancy is not difficult. Starting out in pregnancy with about the correct weight for your build and height is an important beginning. It has been suggested that women who begin pregnancy more than 125 percent of or less than 85 percent of their proper body weight face a greater risk of some abnormality occurring during the pregnancy. This does not mean miscarriages necessarily but all kinds of obstetric difficulties.

The thing about your pre-partum weight that is probably most important is the eating habits you have developed in maintaining that weight. If you eat irregular meals filled with junk foods (empty calories), you will have a more difficult time in keeping up a good diet during pregnancy. It is important to eat balanced meals during pregnancy. Do not diet. Food restriction can be toxic to the developing baby. If you feel fat, diet after you give birth.

Expect to gain between 20 and 25 pounds during your pregnancy. Most of this weight will be put on during the second and third trimesters. Average weight gain is about two pounds per month, but remember that this figure is deceptive since you gain less in the first few months. This added weight is accounted for in the following way (The figures in grams are more precise, since the weights expressed were rounded off to the nearest half pound):

Fetus 7-8 pounds	(3300 grams)
Placenta 1.5 pounds	(650 grams)
Amniotic Fluid 2 pounds	(800 grams)
Enlarged Uterus 2 pounds	(900 grams)
Enlarged Breasts 1 pound	(400 grams)
Expanded Blood Volume	2 1/2 pounds (1250 grams)
Fat	3-10 pounds

Your weight gain should be gradual. Sudden weight gain is a sign of fluid retention, which may be a symptom of toxemia of pregnancy (preeclampsia). The scale only measures pounds; if you develop puffy feet, hands, or face accompanied by sudden weight gain this may be an important sign of a problem. Unless you eat more than 1000 extra calories a day, you will not gain weight suddenly.

During the first trimester you need to eat only 10 more calories per day than you normally do. Ten calories per day is very little, so what we are saying is that during the early part of pregnancy you will need only to be conscious of eating balanced, nutritionally rich meals. Many women take vitamins and iron to make sure that they get enough of these substances to prevent anemia. Other than those replacement nutrients you do not really need to change your diet.

As the infant's bone structure develops, the importance of calcium and vitamin D increases. These nutrients are readily available in milk products. If you do not get enough vitamin D and calcium, they will be pulled from your own bones and teeth and be given to the fetus. By taking in enough of these substances, you prevent harm to your own body.

During the second trimester you need to eat about 100 calories more per day. That is not very much more to add, since about 1 1/2 bananas, or a large slice of cold cut meat, or a third of a cup of tuna fish all have about 100 calories. The important thing to keep track of is the nutritional value of your diet, not the total number of calories.

During the third trimester you will need to add about 300 calories to your daily intake. At this point the baby is big enough to require significant added food stores. And again, any well-balanced diet is acceptable, as long as it includes enough protein, iron, folic acid, calcium, and vitamin D, any balanced set of meals will be adequate.

The following guidelines are stressed by the Committee on Maternal Nutrition of the National Academy of Science and the American College of Obstetricians and Gynecologists:

Iron	30-60 mg of elemental iron supplement per day
Folic acid	400-800 µg supplement per day
Sodium and Iodine	table salt as personally desired; no restriction is necessary.
Calcium	1200 mg per day
Vitamin D	400 IU per day

It has become standard obstetric practice to give women iron supplements and vitamins with folic acid. These replacements are not absolutely necessary if you choose to eat foods that are rich in iron and folic acid. These include liver, kidney, whole grains like brown rice, wheat germ, whole-wheat bread and rolled oats, and green leafy vegetables like spinach, cabbage, and swiss chard. Most women find it hard to get the minimum amount of iron from their diet because they are not used to eating large quantities of these foods. However it can be done, if you are conscientious.

Iron pills are constipating and turn your stool black. For some women this is an inducement to try to get the iron from their regular diet. Some women do not like the idea of taking pills. If you choose to go through your pregnancy without supplements, you should get regular blood counts to test for anemia. This means hematocrit, hemoglobin, and blood indices, which are all obtained from a simple venous blood test. Remember that if you are anemic, the baby will rob your bone marrow of its iron stores, and your anemia will become more severe.

Many women have periods of vomiting, or morning sickness, during pregnancy. Rarely is the vomiting severe enough to endanger the pregnancy. Also most women are able to maintain a normal nutritional intake and weight gain in spite of the nausea and vomiting. This morning sickness is a problem in the first trimester of pregnancy and is thought to be related to the increase in the hormones of pregnancy. It is not a sign of an abnormality that is going to lead to a spontaneous abortion.

Most women are able to maintain adequate nutrition by eating small, frequent, bland meals. Sometimes Bendectin® is used. This is an antihistamine which has some effect on decreasing the vomiting stimulus and on reducing nausea. In addition the Bendectin contains vitamin B^6, which some studies indicate reduces nausea. Only in very severe (and very rare) cases, where no food or liquid can be held in the stomach, is hospitalization and intravenous feeding necessary. For the most part first-trimester morning sickness is not a danger to the pregnancy.

EXERCISE, WORK, AND SEXUALITY

There is no reason to change your exercise or work patterns in order to prevent a recurrence of your spontaneous abortion problem. However, if your work exposes you to chemicals, you may want to be more cautious. No scientific proof demonstrates that you can dislodge a developing embryo by moving. This is true of sexual intercourse as well as work and exercise.

It is quite common to feel fatigued, especially during the early stages of pregnancy. This is not a sign of an abnormal pregnancy, nor is it something you have to feel guilty about. You should rest as much as you need to for your own feeling of well-being. Though this probably has little effect on the likelihood of your carrying the next pregnancy successfully, it is worthwhile because it helps you enjoy life a lot more.

We stated earlier that sexual intercourse—for any length of time and in any position—has no bearing on whether or not you miscarry. You should avoid intercourse only if you experience vaginal bleeding during pregnancy. Many superstitions exist about sexuality and spontaneous abortions, but suffice it to say they are all just superstition based on inadequate scientific understanding.

OTHER RISK FACTORS

It has been known for some time that smoking is related to low birth weight and prematurity in infants. Some say that it can be correlated with spontaneous abortions, but this is not at all clear. In any case it is wise to stop smoking, or at least reduce your intake as much as possible, during pregnancy.

There is also some correlation between spontaneous abortion and becoming pregnant with an IUD in place. Whether the IUD causes an abnormality in the developing fetus or whether it makes proper implantation in the uterus more difficult is again hard to say. As with smoking, hard facts do not exist in this area. It seems wise to have your IUD taken out prior to attempting to conceive and during any medical investigation you may have for recurrent abortion. The IUD can only present an additional unknown to the problem of repeated spontaneous abortions. In any event the IUD must be removed once you become pregnant.

Alcoholism and drug abuse are both dangerous for the baby. Taking any drug during pregnancy, as we discussed in Chapter 5, may be hazardous to the fetus. But the effects of alcohol are particularly destructive. Alcoholic mothers not only addict their babies, but have notoriously bad eating habits; their babies' low birth-weights are the result of the combined effects of poor diet and alcohol. Alcohol abuse increases the risk of congenital malformations. The metabolism of alcohol uses up a great deal of thiamine, so thiamine deficiency is also particularly common.

Similarly, narcotic and street-drug use is very dangerous during pregnancy. No one knows whether heroin users have more spontaneous abortions, but they do have more abnormal infants. Not only is heroin dangerous, but barbiturates, amphetamines and other stimulants, and LSD all are known to cross the placenta. That means that the fetus gets a dose of these substances whenever you take them. Clearly it is wise to abstain during pregnancy.

Hardest of all to assess is the contribution of your emotional state to the success of your pregnancy. Certainly being nervous or upset makes it harder to rest and eat normally. Whether or not this contributes to problems during pregnancy is hard to prove. Some emotional counterpart to illness certainly must exist, especially in relation to nausea. How much it affects you and the baby probably depends on the severity and duration of the problem.

Emotional problems are a risk factor that you should not overlook. If you have had a number of miscarriages, it is reasonable for you to be more anxious than the average couple when you become pregnant. If you do feel nervous, frightened, or depressed, get professional help so that you can deal with these feelings. Be open with your physician about your emotional state. He should be sensitive to what you are feeling as part of his medical management of your pregnancy, but often he will not be. If you have troubles, be open about what you are thinking and feeling. Don't let your problems run away with themselves.

A POSITIVE PERSPECTIVE

An obstetrician we interviewed gave some good advice on how to approach your next pregnancy after having a miscarriage:

> It is very understandable that people should feel that their miscarriage is a major event, especially if they had planned the pregnancy. On the other hand they can appreciate that they will be able to recover from it, just like any other illness like a cold or pneumonia. You will recover and in fact be as good as new. Most pregnancies are normal, and you will have normal children. In fact you are lucky, because this is one of the illnesses you *can* recover from. So you should try to be optimistic.

SUMMARY

1. Invest time and effort in choosing an obstetrician or midwife who is right for you. Be open about all the emotional, medical, and financial issues that are important to you in the area of pregnancy *before* you agree to become that person's patient.
2. Expect to gain 20 to 25 pounds during pregnancy. Most of this weight you gain will be put on in the second and third trimesters of pregnancy. Sudden weight gain may be a sign of toxemia of pregnancy.

3. Proper nutrition requires eating nutritionally balanced meals with an emphasis on the intake of protein, iron, folic acid, calcium, and vitamin D. You do not need to eat a lot of extra calories, just good, wholesome food.

4. It is normal to exercise, work, and have sexual intercourse during pregnancy.

5. Smoking, drugs, and alcohol are potentially hazardous to pregnancy. In addition, if you become pregnant with an IUD in place it should be removed.

6. It is common to feel anxious about your pregnancy if you have had prior miscarriages. If you are worried, depressed, or frightened during your pregnancy, get professional help so that you can work out your feelings.

_____XII_____

Conclusion

A spontaneous abortion is a medical and emotional crisis that affects both of the partners involved profoundly. If there is any single message that we have tried to convey, it is that *if you work things out together, you can overcome your problem and probably have all the children you want.* To do this you need to be open about your feelings, communicate to each other your doubts, frustrations, fears, and anger, and use the strengths of *two* people to sustain your family.

At times when the miscarriage seems most painful, it is worthwhile to remind yourself that what you are experiencing happens to many people. Approximately one in five pregnancies end in spontaneous abortion. Translated into numbers, this means that about 300,000 American couples every year have to bear the same grief and make important adjustments for the future.

Unfortunately, even though miscarriages are so common, they are rarely spoken of, and little has been written that might help the average couple understand the medical and emotional issues that they face. This lack of information prompted us to write this book. We felt that people could profit from the experience of others and learn from the medical facts that were available to doctors but often not conveyed to their patients. It should be comforting to know that your problem is not unique, and that most other couples do go on to have normal, full-term babies.

We have also tried to describe the variation that is normal in the physical process of aborting. This knowledge can be reassuring for the couple who want a perspective on their own miscarriage. Some women undergo long, difficult labor, even with first-trimester abortions. Others have very little discomfort and pass only small amounts of blood and tissue. In some cases the fetus is expelled spontaneously, while other women require a dilation and curettage (D and C) to remove the products of conception. Women who have had multiple abortions, as Chris did, commonly report different physical experiences each time. None of this is particularly useful in determining why you miscarried (unless it is a question of an incompetent cervix, which happens late in pregnancy) or predicting your ability to carry your next pregnancy to term.

The sense of emotional loss, however, is universal, and we have tried to give you an idea of how other women and men have responded to spontaneous abortions by presenting their stories in their own words. A miscarriage is a sudden, unexpected, and shocking loss of life. It shatters your hopes for children and fills you with doubts about the future. For anyone who feels that it is important to have a family, this can be one of life's great disappointments and it is normal to have many strong and unpleasant emotions associated with it.

Some people find it easier than others to express their

feelings during these times of stress. We believe that expressing those feelings to each other is an important part of getting through the crisis and promoting growth in your own relationship. Unfortunately in some ways this society places taboos on discussing sadness and loss, and so we are reluctant to say openly what we feel. However, it is difficult to face both the present and the future unless you confront these issues together. Often it is harder for men to admit these emotions. There still are sexual stereotypes that equate sadness with weakness for men. In spite of this, men should be aware that grieving is a necessary part of the process by which we readjust to the normal routine of life after a personal tragedy. Moreover, we seem to have lost some of the structured ways of grieving that still exist in other societies. These customs often make it easier to work out the emotions that arise from personal loss. You should remind yourselves that it is important to admit the sadness of the miscarriage openly to each other and look to your collective strength in working out your grief.

It is frustrating for many couples that there is not a better scientific understanding of why spontaneous abortions occur. We do know that about half of the aborted fetuses that have been studied were genetically abnormal. This fact led us to the theory that a miscarriage is nature's mechanism for preventing the birth of abnormal infants. This is only a theory and does not explain why these abnormal fetuses are conceived or begin to develop. Our current understanding indicates that most of the time these events are genetic accidents that occur on a chance basis and therefore may or may not occur with your next pregnancy. It does not explain why some women have several abortions before carrying a pregnancy to term, while others never abort. It should be reassuring for you to know that the fetus you aborted was likely to have been abnormal, even though our medical knowledge of why it was abnormal is rather unclear.

In our explanation of the genetics of spontaneous abortion we tried to emphasize that it is chance that causes most of these abnormalities. Because of this it is likely that your succeeding pregnancies will be normal. Only a small number of couples carry a genetic error (translocation) that is repeatedly passed on during conception. This is another fact from which to gather hope. We believe that it is wise for couples who have experienced repeated spontaneous abortions to have their chromosomes analyzed. Once you find out that your chromosomes are normal, you can be more hopeful that your subsequent pregnancies are likely to succeed.

A further source of frustration is that there is no widely accepted method of treatment for a threatened abortion. In the past various drugs were administered in an effort to sustain pregnancy. Most doctors now feel that the risks involved outweigh the potential benefits. Bed rest is often recommended when a woman is bleeding during pregnancy, but this treatment is based on tradition rather than a sound medical understanding of the problem. We do not know if bed rest helps during a threatened abortion, but it is not likely to be harmful.

Because we lack effective methods of treatment for spontaneous abortion, it is easy to become angry with physicians and with medicine as a whole. However, it is important not to expect magical solutions from unorthodox treatments or avant-garde medical practitioners. As consumers of medical services you should also be wary about extensive and expensive medical testing. We just do not know many of the answers, and it is highly unlikely that any one physician will have developed a treatment that no other physician is aware of. We have become increasingly aware in recent years that it is often best to allow the natural process of conception and pregnancy to occur without interference. The high incidence of cancers of the reproductive organs among children born to women who took DES (diethylstilbestrol) during pregnancy is an example of how dangerous it can be to interfere with the pregnancy process.

In general, be discerning when you receive medical advice, ask questions about your medical care, and consider only those tests and procedures which seem appropriate to your problem. Avoid drugs whenever possible during pregnancy. Although our knowledge in this area is limited, we do know that most drugs do cross the placenta and enter the fetus. When in doubt obtain other medical opinions. Invest time and effort in choosing an obstetrician or midwife who is right for you. This will be important throughout the time that you are undergoing medical testing and during your pregnancy.

This is a book that has a happy ending. Chris and Mark, like most couples who suffer miscarriages, were able to have their child during the writing of this book. Having three miscarriages in three years was hard, but it added to their knowledge of each other and catalyzed individual personal growth. It caused them both to reexamine their feelings about the things that they valued, and made them more appreciative of their own strengths as a family. There are many problems in life that unfortunately are not so amenable to persistence as the problem of spontaneous abortion. In this area repeated effort is likely to produce a normal child.

Each experience in life is an opportunity for growth. Many of the important things in life are accomplished through struggle and persistence and, once they are attained, give added satisfaction because of the effort they demanded. That applies to having a family as well as to other endeavors. Living as a productive family member is a constantly demanding role. It changes over time, but the intensity of the involvement and the commitment to the task is an ongoing challenge.

References

ALBERMAN, E. ET AL. Previous reproductive history in mothers presenting with spontaneous abortion. *Br. J. of Obstet. Gynecol.*, 82, 366-373, May 1975.

AWAN, A. Some biologic correlates of pregnancy wastage. *Am. J. Ob. Gyn.*, 119, 4, 525-532, Jun 15, 1974.

BEISCHER, N. AND MACKAY E. *Obstetrics and the Newborn*. Saunders: Philadelphia, 1977.

BICKLEY, H. *Practical concepts in human disease*. Williams and Wilkins: Baltimore, 1974.

BLOOM, A.D. ET AL. Cytogenetics of the in utero exposed of Hiroshima and Nagasaki. *Lancet*, 2, 10-12, 1968.

BOUE, J. AND BOUE, A. Chromosomal analysis of two consecutive abortuses in each of 43 women. *Humangenetik*, 19, 275-280, 1973.

BOUE, J. ET AL. The epidemiology of human spontaneous abortion with chromosomal abnormalities. In *Aging gametes*, Blandau, R.J. ed., pp. 330-348. Karger, Basel, 1975.

BOUE, J. ET AL. Outcome of pregnancies following a spontaneous abortion with chromosomal anomalies. *Am. J. Ob. Gyn.*, 116, 6, 806-811, Jul, 1973.

BRAUNSTEIN, G. ET AL. Subclinical spontaneous abortion. *Obstet. Gynecol.*, 50, 1, 41-44 (supplement), Jul 1977.

BURROW, G.N. The thyroid gland in pregnancy. Saunders: Philadelphia, 1972.

CARR, D.H. Chromosomes and abortion. *Adv. Hum. Genet.*, 2, 201-257, 1971.

CARR, D.H. Chromosome anomalies as a cause of spontaneous abortion. *Am. J. Ob. Gyn.* 97, 3, 283-293, Feb 1967.

CARR, D. ET AL. Chromosome studies in selected spontaneous abortions: unusual cytogenetic disorders. *Teratology*, 5, 49-55, Feb 1972.

CHARD, T. ET AL. Risks of amniocentesis. *N.Eng. J. Med.*, 299, 2, 101, Jul 13, 1978.

COLLMAN, R. D. ET AL. Incidence of infectious hepatitis compared with the incidence of children with Down's syndrome born nine months later to younger and older mothers. *J. Ment. Def. Res.*, 10, 266, 1966.

CONSUMER REPORTS. Cutting the risk of childbirth after 35. 44, 5, 302-306, May 1979.

DANFORTH, DAVID. *Obstetrics and Gynecology*. Harper & Row: Hagerstown, Maryland, 1977.

FAIRWEATHER, D. Techniques and safety of amniocentesis, in *Amniotic fluid: Research and clinical application*. Fairweather and Eskes, eds. Excerpta Medica: Amsterdam, 1978.

FEDRICK, J. ADELSTERIN, P. Area differences in the incidence of neural tube defects and the rate of spontaneous abortion. *Brit. J. Prev. Soc. Med.*, 30, 32-35, 1976.

FRENCH ET AL. Probabilities of fetal mortality. *Public Health Reports*, 77, 10, 835-847, Oct 1972.

GLASS, R.H. AND M. GOLBUS Habitual abortion. *Fertil. Steril.*, 29, 3, Mar 1978.

GORDON, Y.B. ET AL. Foetal wastage as a result of an alpha feto protein screening program. *Lancet*, 1, 677-678, 1978.

HEXTER, WILLIAM, YOST, HENRY. *The science of genetics*. Prentice Hall: Englewood Cliffs, N.J., 1976.

HILL, R.B. Drugs ingested by pregnant women. *Clinical Pharmacology and Therapeutics*, 14, 654, 1973.

JAMES, W.H. The problem of spontaneous abortion X. The efficiency of psychotherapy. *Am. J. Ob. Gyn.*, 85, 38, 1963.

JONES, G. AND E. DELFS. Endocrine patterns in term pregnancies following abortion. *JAMA*, 146, 1212, 1951.

KAJII, T. ET AL. Banding analysis of abnormal karyotypes in spontaneous abortion. *Am. J. Hum. Genet.*, 25, 539-547, 1973.

KIM, H. ET AL. Cytogenetics of fetal wastage. *N. Eng. J. Med.*, 293, 17, 844-47, Oct 23 1975.

KIMBALL, A.C. ET AL. The role of toxoplasmosis in abortion. *Am. J. Ob. Gyn.*, 111, 219, 1971.

LANDESMAN, R. ET AL. Detection of human chorionic gonadotropin in blood of regularly bleeding women using copper intrauterine contraceptive devices. *Fertil. Steril.*, 27, 9, 1062-1066, Sept 1976.

LAURITSEN, J.G. Aetiology of spontaneous abortion. *Acta Obstet. et Gynecol. Scand.*, Suppl 52, 1-29, 1976.

LAURITSEN, J.G. Genetic aspects of spontaneous abortion. *Danish Med. Bull.*, 24, 5, 169-188, Oct 77.

LAURITSEN, J.G. The significance of oral contraceptives in causing chromosome anomalies in spontaneous abortions. *Acta Obstet. et Gynecol. Scand.*, 54, 261, 1975.

MANN, E.G. Psychiatric investigation of habitual abortion. *Obstet. Gynecol.*, 7, 589, 1956.

MOODY, PAUL. *Genetics of Man*. Norton: New York, 1967.

NORA, A.H, NORA, J.J. A syndrome of multiple congenital anomalies associated with teratogenic exposure. *Arch. Environ. Health*, 30, 17, 1975.

PEETERS, L. ET AL. Serum levels of human placental lactogen and human chorionic gonadotropin in early pregnancy: A maturational index of the placenta. *Am. J. Ob. Gyn.*, 126, 6, 707-711, Nov 1976.

POLAND, M. Embryonic development in patients with recurrent abortions. *Fertil. Steril.*, 22, 5, 325-331, May 1971.

REID, D. ET AL. *Principles and Management of Human Reproduction.* Saunders: Phila, 1972, p. 255.

ROCKLIN, R. ET AL. Maternal-fetal relation. *N. Eng. J. Med.*, 295, 1, 209-213, Nov 25, 1976.

ROSAL, T. ET AL. Application of a radio-receptor assay of human chorionic gonadotropin in the diagnosis of early abortion. *Fertil. Steril.*, 26, 11, 1105-1112, Nov 1975.

SCHEINFELD, A. *Heredity in humans.* Lippincott: New York, 1972.

SHAPIRO, S. ET AL. Factors associated with early and late fetal loss. Reprinted from *Excerpta Medica International Congress Series*, No. 224, American Association of Planned Parenthood, VIIth Annual Meeting, Boston, April 1970.

STEIN, A. ET AL. Spontaneous abortion as a screening device: the effect of fetal survival on the incidence of birth defects. *Am. J. Epidemiol.*, 102, 4, 275-290, 1975.

STERN, C. Principles of human genetics. Freeman: San Francisco, 1973.

TAYLOR, W. The probability of fetal death. In *Lifetable, Incidences from congenital malformations*, Fraser, C. & V. McKusick, eds. *Excerpta Medica:* New York, 1969.

TUPPER, C., WEIL, R.J. The problem of spontaneous abortion IX. The treatment of habitual aborters by psychotherapy. *Am. J. Ob. Gyn.*, 85, 38, 1963.

WARBURTON, D, FRASER, F.C. Spontaneous abortion risks in man: data from reproductive histories collected in a medical genetics unit. *Human Genetics*, 16, 1, 1-23, Mar 1964.

YOUNG, P. ET AL. Amniocentesis antenatal diagnosis. Review of problems and outcomes in a large series. *Am. J. Ob. Gyn.*, 125, 495-501, 1976.

GLOSSARY

ABORTION (SPONTANEOUS)—Termination of pregnancy prior to the time that the fetus can live on its own.

ABORTUS—Aborted fetus

AMNIOCENTESIS—Procedure for obtaining amniotic fluid during pregnancy. Useful for genetic analysis of the fetus.

AMNIOTIC SAC—Cavity formed during pregnancy by the amniotic membrane. This sac ("bag of waters") encloses and protects the fetus.

AMPHETAMINE—A drug that stimulates the central nervous system. Commonly called "speed," it increases metabolism and heart rate, and affects the fetus as well as many other organs in the body.

ANTIBIOTICS—Substances produced by a living organism (e.g. mold) or synthetically manufactured, which can eradicate or arrest the growth of pathological bacteria and fungi that attack humans.

ASHERMAN'S SYNDROME—Uterine adhesions produced by post-abortion infection or overly vigorous curettage of the uterus.

AUTOIMMUNE DISEASE—Disease process in which the body's own defense system acts against its own tissues, thereby causing damage to itself.

BACTERIA—One-celled microorganisms. Some bacteria live in harmony with the human body, while some are capable of causing disease.

BASAL BODY TEMPERATURE—Morning temperature, obtained after a restful sleep, which measures the basic rate of body metabolism. Can be used to follow the female menstrual cycle, since temperature changes occur on a rhythmic basis in response to hormone changes.

BIOPSY—Surgical removal of a small amount of tissue for microscopic analysis.

BLASTOCYST—Early stage of the embryo in which the trophoblastic cells have formed.

CERVIX—Neck of the uterus.

CHROMOSOMES—Genetic material contained in the nucleus of a cell, responsible for transmission of hereditary information and for control of cellular metabolism.

CLOMID®—(clomiphene) A pituitary stimulant which when given to humans improves ovulation and promotes functioning of the corpus luteum.

CONCEPTION—Fertilization; union of egg and sperm to create a new life.

CONE BIOPSY (conization of the cervix)—Surgical removal of a cone-shaped wedge of abnormal tissue from the cervix for microscopic analysis. When the abnormality is superficial, complete cone biopsy can be curative, in that it will remove the entire abnormality.

CORPUS LUTEUM—Small, yellow body in the ovary responsible for progesterone production.

CYTOMEGALOVIRUS—A herpeslike virus found in human saliva, urine, and cervical secretions. It is thought that this virus can affect the newborn and might be responsible for pregnancy loss, although this is not fully substantiated.

D AND C (dilation and curettage)—Expansion of the cervix, followed by the insertion of a spoon-shaped instrument for scraping the inner lining of the uterus. It is performed to obtain tissue samples for analysis, to stop bleeding during hemorrhage, and to remove retained products of conception.

DOWN'S SYNDROME (mongolism)—A birth abnormality with characteristic facial and other physical characteristics, and differing levels of mental retardation.

ECTOPIC PREGNANCY—Implantation of the fertilized egg outside of the uterus.

EFFACEMENT—The obliteration of the cervical os during labor due to the thinning and stretching of the tissue.

EMBRYO—A fertilized ovum, or conceptus of 2 to 8 weeks of gestation.

ENDOCRINE—Internal secretions from glands that help regulate body functions.

ENDOMETRIUM—Lining of the inner surface of the uterus.

EROSION—Destruction of the surface layer of tissue due to injury or infection.

ETIOLOGY—The cause of a medical abnormality or disease.

FALLOPIAN TUBE—Named after the Italian anatomist, Fallopius, the tube or conduit that carries the ovum (egg) from the ovary to the uterus.

FERTILIZATION—Penetration of the sperm into the ovum (egg) to create a new life.

FETUS—Intrauterine life from 9 weeks until birth.

FUNDUS—Body of the uterus.

GAMMA GLOBULIN—Protein substance formed in the blood which is active in the body's resistance to infection.

GENE—Subsections of the chromosome responsible for carrying inherited traits.

GRAFT—See TRANSPLANT

HABITUAL ABORTION—Repeated spontaneous abortion.

HERPES SIMPLEX VIRUS—Virus capable of causing blister-like eruptions of the skin of the face, mouth, and/or genitals. The eruption appears as a fluid-filled sac on a red base.

HORMONE—A chemical produced and secreted into the blood which stimulates one or many target organs (e.g. uterus, ovary, skin). Hormones regulate reproduction.

HUMAN CHORIONIC GONADOTROPIN (HCG)—A hormone produced early in pregnancy which appears to be integral to maintaining normal gestation. It is also useful for diagnosis of pregnancy.

HYSTEROSALPINGOGRAM—X-ray examination of the uterus and Fallopian tubes.

IDIOGRAM—A picture of the human chromosomes made during laboratory examination.

IMMUNOGLOBULIN—Protein substances found in the blood important for defense against disease.

IMMUNOLOGICAL—Pertaining to the body's natural defenses against disease.

INCOMPETENT CERVIX—Weakened cervix that is unable to maintain itself during pregnancy.

INTRAMUSCULAR INJECTION—An injection into the muscle.

INTRAUTERINE DEVICE (IUD)—Coil or other material inserted into the uterus to prevent conception.

KARYOTYPE—Picture of the human chromosomes for genetic analysis (idiogram).

LYMPHOCYTE—One of the white cells of the blood, important for maintenance of the body's defenses against disease and useful for studying genetic abnormalities.

MEIOSIS—Cell division by which sperm and egg are produced. During this process the new cells formed have half the original number of chromosomes.

MISCARRIAGE—Spontaneous abortion of a fetus.

MITOSIS—Cell division by which new cells are produced for human growth and for replacement of dying or dead cells. In this process the new cells have the full number of chromosomes.

MORULA—Ball of cells formed early in the life of the fertilized ovum.

MYCOPLASMA—A microscopic parasite of man known to cause respiratory infections and thought to be responsible for pregnancy loss.

MYOMA—A tumor or swelling of muscle tissue.

NEURAL TUBE DEFECT—Birth defect of the brain and/or spinal cord.

NIDATION—Implantation (nesting) of the fertilized egg in the uterus.

NUCLEUS—The vital center of the cell, which controls reproduction and cell regulation.

OOCYTE—Primitive form of the ovum, or egg.

OVA—Reproductive cells of the female. Plural of ovum.

OVARY—Female organs responsible for production of sex hormones and eggs (ova).

OVULATION—Process by which a mature egg is produced.

PELVIC EXAM—Medical examination of the vagina, uterus, ovaries, and adjacent structures.

PELVIC INFLAMMATORY DISEASE (PID)—Infection and inflammation of the pelvic organs and adjacent structures.

PLACENTA—The oval, spongy vascular organ that supplies the fetus with maternal blood and nutrients.

POLYP—A swelling or protrusion attached by a stem to the cervix, rectum, nose, larynx or other structure. .

PROGESTERONE—A female hormone important during pregnancy and menstruation.

RH DISEASE (Erythroblastosis fetalis)—A disease in which the mother's sensitized immune system crosses the placenta and attacks the red blood cells of the fetus.

RUBELLA (German measles)—A viral disease characterized by fever, rash, inflammation of the throat, and headache of short duration. Most important is the potential damage to the fetus if the infection occurs in the pregnant mother.

SAC OF PREGNANCY—Amniotic sac.

SPECULUM—Instrument for examining the vagina.

SPERM—Male sex cells; semen.

TERATOGEN—Agent capable of causing birth abnormalities.

THREATENED ABORTION—Bleeding, cramping, dilation of the cervix, or other abnormality during pregnancy signaling a potential miscarriage.

TOTIPOTENTIAL—A cell capable of differentiating itself into one of many different types of cells.

TRANSLOCATION (Balanced)—Abnormal rearrangement of genetic material during cell division.

TRANSPLANT—Incorporation of tissue from a donor (outside source) into the body of a recipient.

TRENDELENBURG POSITION—Position in which the person lies on their back, with the bed tilted, so that the knees and hips are above the head.

TROPHOBLAST—Outermost layer of the blastocyst form of the developing fertilized egg.

ULTRASOUND—A laboratory test that uses high-energy sound waves to electrically visualize the uterus and its contents.

UTERUS (Womb)—Female organ of reproduction that contains and nourishes the developing fetus.

VAGINA—Muscular organ of the female that forms a passageway between the vulva and uterus.

VIRUS—Microscopic particle capable of causing disease in humans. It differs from bacteria in that it cannot live on its own, but must reside inside the cell of another organism.

WASTAGE (Fetal)—Death or damage to the fetus.

Index

More Reading from SIGNET and MENTOR

Self-Help Books from SIGNET

**Buy them at your local
bookstore or use coupon
on next page for ordering.**

Staying Healthy with SIGNET Books